GAMES FOR YOUR ZX SPECTRUM

GAMES FOR YOUR ZX SPECTRUM

By
Peter Shaw

First published in Great Britain in 1983 by Virgin Books Ltd, 61-63 Portobello Road,London W11 3DD.

Copyright © 1983 Interface/Virgin Books

ISBN 0 907080 84 7

Printed and bound in Great Britain by Richard Clay (The Chaucer Press) Ltd, Suffolk.

Production services by Book Production Consultants, Cambridge.

Designed by Ray Hyden.

Illustrated by Sue Walliker.

Typeset by Portobello Typesetting.

Distributed by Hamlyn Paperbacks.

TO SUE POWELL

TIM HARTNELL — SERIES EDITOR

Tim Hartnell is a leading computer expert and journalist, who has contributed extensively to the Technical Consumer Press. He is also the author of several books including *Getting Acquainted With Your ZX81*, *Let Your BBC Micro Teach You to Program* and *Programming Your ZX Spectrum*.

PETER SHAW — THE AUTHOR

Peter Shaw is a 16-year-old schoolboy who has contributed to *Interface* magazine and to *ZX Computing*. More recently he played the Dame in the Christmas pantomime at school.

SUE WALLIKER — THE ILLUSTRATOR

Sue Walliker is a freelance illustrator.

ACKNOWLEDGEMENTS

The author would like to thank Maureen Gates for all her help in the writing of this book; Alan Dennis, Steven Gunning and Michael Merrifield for their ideas for programs; and Tim Hartnell and Clive Gifford for their support. Special thanks must go to Mark and David Palmer who, in their own small way, helped make this book possible.

CONTENTS

Editor's Introduction

Your computer is waiting to challenge you. Moving graphics games, brain stretchers, word games and puzzles are all here and ready to entertain you.

A wide variety of games are included in this book. The programs have been written by some of the most talented young programmers working in this country at the moment, and represent a variety of approaches to solving programming problems.

An examination of the listings should teach you many tricks and techniques to apply to your own programming. And once you have mastered the programs in their present form, you might want to try your hand at improving them. There is no such thing as a 'perfect program', so these games are sure to benefit from your programming skill.

All that now remains is for you to turn the page and enter the programs. I can only hope that you enjoy playing the games as much as we did when preparing this volume.

Tim Hartnell, series editor
London
March 1983

Author's Introduction

The Spectrum is an amazing computer; by comparison its little brother the ZX81 is slow and crude, since the only way of playing a Space Invader type game is to delve into machine code. The Spectrum offers the convenience of programming arcade games in BASIC.

The programs in this book consist mainly of games. I have steered away from the stocking fillers such as Biorhythms or Sketchpad, not because I have anything against these programs, just that they seem to crop up in most micro magazines regularly.

Once you have typed in these programs don't stop there — improve on them. If you find a user-defined character which you think could do with a bit of slimming down, then change it!

Pete Shaw
Stanwell, Middlesex
November, 1982

Programming Skills and Techniques

Most of my programs start with a familiar layout:

10 REM Program name
20 GOSUB 9000: REM UDGs
30 GOSUB 8000: REM Variables
40 GOSUB 7000: REM Draw Screen

Apart from making it easier to add lines when the computer is given a GO TO command, the computer searches from line one until it finds the line. When writing an arcade or action game — where speed is essential — this method of subroutining fractionally accelerates movement.

Hints and Tips

The Spectrum has a number of hidden secrets which are not apparently obvious in the instruction manual, and some are not even mentioned. The hash symbol (#) can be used in PRINT statements to print in various positions on the screen:

PRINT# 1; "This is printed in the lower part of the screen": PAUSE Ø

As you can see # 1 prints in the lower half of the screen, making a 24 line display possible.

ZX computers are the only micros that I can think of which can only INPUT at the bottom of the screen;

however, with the use of INPUT AT you can INPUT information anywhere you like on the screen:

> INPUT AT 22,0; AT 0,0; "What is your name ";
> LINE a$; AT 10,0; "What is your age "; (a$);
> " ";a;AT 15,0;(a$); "'s age is ";a;AT 20,0;"Press
> ENTER to continue";b$

There are a number of disadvantages with this method. Firstly, as you can see, the length of the lines are a problem; and, secondly, the BORDER colour has to be the same as the PAPER colour since the lower half of the screen is extended to nearly all of the top part. (I say nearly because it leaves one strip of the upper part of the screen which is clearly visible unless the paper and border colours are the same.)

Throughout this book I have attempted to use UDGs wherever possible. My main help was a product called the 'Print 'n' Plotter Jotter'. This is a pad with two grids on each page, the bottom grid is 32 x 22, and is useful for planning out displays. The top grid is 64 x 44 and is the grid I use for defining my characters. You could use graph paper, but the squares are so small that UDGs become fiddly, and hard to define.

EGG SAVIOUR

In this game you are the Egg Saviour, and your task is to save poor, helpless eggs from the clutches of evil, tyrannical powers which restrain your movement by firing laser beams. You collect the eggs by running into the 'X' below the egg boxes at the top of the screen; once you have picked up the eggs your man will turn green. You must negotiate the laser beams and put the egg in your egg box by running over the '-'. When you have collected half a dozen eggs you get 100 points and a new screenful of eggs.

There are a number of rules to this game:

1. You cannot run over anything apart from the 'X' or '-'; if you do then you lose a life.
2. If you are hit by a laser, or lose a life in any other way, then you automatically lose the egg you are carrying; if you are not carrying an egg then you only lose a life.
3. You can only carry one egg at a time; if you are carrying an egg and try to pick up another by running over an 'X', then the 'X' will disappear, making it impossible to pick up the egg in the egg box above the 'X'.
4. You have three lives, which last about ten seconds when you first play the game, although with practice you can reach a reasonable score.

Use the cursor keys to control your movement.

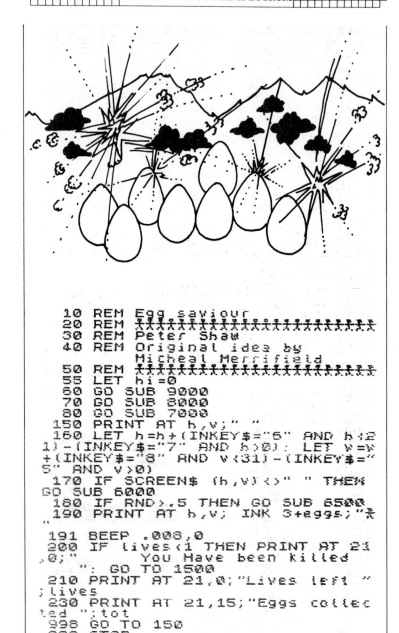

```
  10 REM Egg saviour
  20 REM ♀♂♀♂♀♂♀♂♀♂♀♂♀♂♀♂♀♂♀♂
  30 REM Peter Shaw
  40 REM Original idea by
         Micheal Merrifield
  50 REM ♀♂♀♂♀♂♀♂♀♂♀♂♀♂♀♂♀♂♀♂
  55 LET hi=0
  60 GO SUB 9000
  70 GO SUB 8000
  80 GO SUB 7000
 150 PRINT AT h,v;" "
 160 LET h=h+(INKEY$="6" AND h<2
1)-(INKEY$="7" AND h>0): LET v=v
+(INKEY$="8" AND v<31)-(INKEY$="
5" AND v>0)
 170 IF SCREEN$ (h,v)<>" " THEN
GO SUB 6000
 180 IF RND>.5 THEN GO SUB 8500
 190 PRINT AT h,v; INK 3+eggs;"是
"
 191 BEEP .008,0
 200 IF lives<1 THEN PRINT AT 23
,0;"      You Have been killed
    ": GO TO 1500
 210 PRINT AT 21,0;"Lives left "
;lives
 230 PRINT AT 21,15;"Eggs collec
ted ";tot
 998 GO TO 150
 999 STOP
```

```
1500 BEEP 1,4: BEEP 1,4: BEEP .3
,4: BEEP 1.2,4: BEEP .75,7: BEEP
 .5,6: BEEP 1,6: BEEP .3,4: BEEP
 .7,4: BEEP .5,3: BEEP 1,4
1501 IF sc>hi THEN LET hi=sc
1510 INPUT "Press ENTER to play
again "; LINE a$: CLS : GO TO 70
2000 IF eggs=1 THEN RETURN
2005 PRINT AT 1,v;"   ";AT 2,v; I
NK 6;"▗▖"
2010 LET eggs=1
2015 BEEP .1,10
2020 RETURN
2500 IF eggs=0 THEN PRINT AT h,v
; INK 1;"-": LET h=h+1: RETURN
2510 PRINT AT 17,v; INK 6;"▲";A
T 18,v; OVER 1; INK 6;"▼"
2515 LET eggs=0
2516 PRINT AT 19,v;" "
2517 BEEP .1,20: BEEP .15,15
2520 LET tot=tot+1: IF tot=6 THE
N GO TO 9500
2530 RETURN
6000 LET b$=SCREEN$ (h,v)
6010 IF b$="X" THEN GO TO 2000
6020 IF b$="-" THEN GO TO 2500
6030 LET lives=lives-1
6031 LET eggs=0
6040 PRINT AT h,v; FLASH 1; INK
3;"⚡": BEEP .1,-10: FOR p=1 TO 2
0: NEXT p: RETURN
6500 GO TO (INT (RND*3)+1)*100+6
500
6600 PLOT 9,m1: DRAW INK 2; BRIG
HT 1;245,0
6605 GO SUB 6900
6606 PAUSE 2
6610 DRAW OVER 1;-248,0: PLOT OV
ER 1;254,m1: RETURN
6700 PLOT m2,167: DRAW INK 2; BR
IGHT 1;0,-120
6705 GO SUB 6900
6706 PAUSE 2
6710 DRAW OVER 1;0,120: RETURN
6800 PLOT m3,167: DRAW INK 2; BR
IGHT 1;0,-120
6805 GO SUB 6900
6806 PAUSE 2
6810 DRAW OVER 1;0,120: RETURN
6900 IF SCREEN$ (h,v)<>" " THEN
GO TO 6000
6910 RETURN
7000 LET n=0: PRINT AT 0,0;"Scor
e ";sc;TAB 23;"High ";hi
7005 FOR a=1 TO 4
```

```
7010 PRINT AT 1,n;"    ";
7020 FOR b=1 TO e(a)
7030 PRINT INK 6;" ▲ ";
7040 NEXT b
7050 PRINT AT 2,n;"   ";
7060 FOR b=1 TO e(a)
7070 PRINT INK 6;" ▼ ";
7080 NEXT b
7090 OVER 1
7095 PRINT AT 2,n;"   ";
7100 FOR b=1 TO e(a)
7110 PRINT INK 6;"⊔";
7120 NEXT b
7122 PRINT AT 3,n;"   ";
7125 FOR b=1 TO e(a): PRINT INK
6;"X ";: NEXT b
7130 LET n=n+(e(a)*2)+2
7140 NEXT a
7150 PRINT AT 0,9; INK 2;"▼";AT
0,21;"▼";AT 4,0;"►"
7160 PRINT AT 18,8; INK 1;"⊔ ⊔
⊔ ⊔ ⊔"
7165 PRINT AT 19,8; INK 1;"-
-   -   -"
7170 OVER 0
7990 RETURN
8000 BORDER 0: INK 7: PAPER 0: C
LS
8010 DIM e(4)
8020 RESTORE 9120: FOR z=1 TO 4:
 READ e(z): NEXT z
8030 LET h=10: LET v=15
8040 LET sc=0: RANDOMIZE
8060 LET m1=17*8+4: LET m2=9*8+4
: LET m3=21*8+4
8070 LET eggs=0
8080 LET lives=3
8090 LET tot=0
8100 RETURN
8989 REM *********************
8990 REM   Graphics characters
8991 REM      ● Graphic ab
8992 REM        Graphic cd
8993 REM     ⊔ Graphic ef
8994 REM      ≛ Graphic g
8995 REM     ► Graphic h
8996 REM     ▼ Graphic i
8997 REM *********************
```

18

```
9000 FOR a=USR "a" TO USR "j"-1
9010 READ user: POKE a,user
9020 NEXT a: RETURN
9030 DATA 1,3,7,7,15,15,15,31
9040 DATA 128,192,224,224,240,24
0,248,248
9050 DATA 31,31,31,31,15,15,7,3
9060 DATA 248,248,248,248,240,24
0,224,192
9070 DATA 192,192,192,192,192,22
4,224,255
9080 DATA 3,3,3,3,3,7,7,255
9090 DATA 56,56,16,254,16,16,40,
68
9100 DATA 128,192,240,255,255,24
0,192,128
9110 DATA 255,126,60,60,60,24,24
,24
9111 REM ***************************
9120 DATA 3,2,2,3
9500 LET sc=sc+100
9505 LET h=10: LET v=15: LET tot
=0: LET eggs=0
9510 PRINT AT 0,0;"Score ";sc
9515 IF sc>hi THEN LET hi=sc
9520 FOR p=1 TO 31: BEEP .01,p:
BEEP .006,-p: NEXT p
9530 CLS
9540 GO TO 80
```

Lives left 1   Eggs collected 2

Lives left 1   Eggs collected 2

You Have been killed

BOX BOUNCE

In this game you must keep the ball bouncing around the screen; you score points when you successfully bounce the ball off your bat (the square at the bottom of the screen). If, however, the ball hits the square on the side then you lose a life. You have three lives and I defy you to beat my top score of 20. Use key 5 to move left and key 8 to move right.

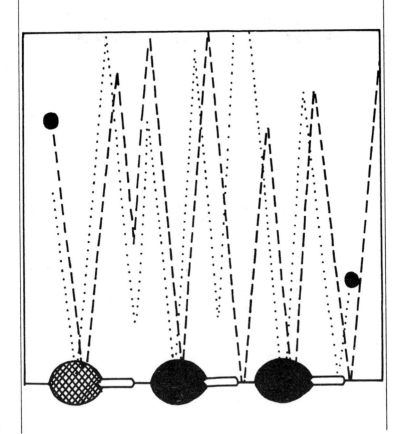

21

Score 2   Lives left 3

Score 6   Lives left 1

Score 2   Lives left 3

```
   10 REM box-bounce
   20 REM Peter Shaw
   30 REM Original idea by
         Alan Dennis
   40 LET hi=0
   50 GO SUB 9000
   60 GO SUB 8000
   65 PRINT AT 21,15;"Lives left
";lives
   70 PRINT AT 20,v;" "
   80 LET v=v+(INKEY$="8" AND v<5
1)-(INKEY$="5" AND v>0)
   85 LET v=v+2*(INKEY$=CHR$ 9 AN
D v<31)-2*(INKEY$=CHR$ 8 AND v>0
)
   90 PRINT AT 20,v; INK 5; BRIGH
T 1;"□"
  100 PRINT AT a,b;" "
```

```
 110 LET a=a+m: IF a>19 OR a<1 T
HEN BEEP .05,10: LET m=-m
 120 LET b=b+n: IF b>30 OR b<1 T
HEN BEEP .05,15: LET n=-n
 130 PRINT AT a,b; INK c;"●"
 140 IF a=0 OR a=20 THEN PRINT A
T a,b; INK c;"●"
 150 IF b=0 OR b=31 THEN PRINT A
T a,b; INK c;"●"
 160 IF a=19 AND b=v THEN PRINT
AT a,b; INK c;"●": BEEP .05,15:
LET sc=sc+2: LET m=-m
 170 IF a=20 AND b=v THEN GO SUB
500
 180 PRINT AT 21,0;"Score ";sc
 190 GO TO 70
 500 PRINT AT 20,v; FLASH 1; INK
2;"□"
 510 LET lives=lives-1
 515 PRINT AT 21,15;"Lives left
";lives
 520 FOR p=1 TO 20: BEEP .008,-p
: NEXT p
 525 IF lives=0 THEN GO TO 600
 526 LET a=INT (RND*5)+2: LET b=
INT (RND*27)+2
 530 RETURN
 600 PRINT AT 2,10; FLASH 1; BRI
GHT 1;"GAME OVER"
 610 PRINT '''"          You scor
ed ";sc
 620 IF sc>hi THEN LET hi=sc
 630 PRINT '''"       Highest score
 today ";hi
 640 INPUT "Press ENTER to play
again       "; LINE a$: GO TO 50
8000 BORDER 1: PAPER 0: INK 7: C
LS
8005 LET v=15: LET a=INT (RND*5)
+2: LET b=INT (RND*27)+2
8010 LET sc=0: LET m=1: LET n=1
8020 LET c=6: LET lives=3
8990 RETURN
9000 FOR a=USR "a" TO USR "d"+7
9010 READ user: POKE a,user
9020 NEXT a: RETURN
9030 DATA 60,126,255,255,255,255
,126,60
9040 DATA 0,0,0,60,126,255,126,6
0
9050 DATA 8,28,62,62,62,62,28,8
9060 DATA 255,129,129,129,129,12
9,129,255
```

23

NESSIE

This game is a variation of Duckshoot in which your targets swim across the screen above you. You score points by shooting them, and the more you can shoot down the more points you will gain. There is a bonus should you be able to clear a whole row. Use key 5 to go left, 8 to go right and Ø to fire.

BONUS 2000 POINTS

SCORE 3160   MISSILES 0

GAME OVER

You scored 3160

Highest score today 3160

```
  10 REM NESSIE
  20 LET hi=0: GO SUB 9000
  30 GO SUB 8000
  40 LET s=0: LET mis=20: GO SUB
7000
  50 PRINT AT 5,0;a$''b$
  60 LET h=h+(INKEY$="8" AND h<3
0)-(INKEY$="5" AND h>0)
  70 IF INKEY$="0" THEN LET mis=
mis-1: GO SUB 1000
  75 IF mis<1 THEN GO TO 500
  80 PRINT AT 20,h; INK 6;"
"
  90 LET b$=b$(2 TO )+b$(1)
 100 LET a$=a$(LEN a$)+a$( TO (L
EN a$)-1)
 101 PRINT AT 0,0; PAPER 5; INK
0;"SCORE ";s,"MISSILES ";mis;" "
 110 IF b$="
             " THEN GO SUB 2000
 120 IF a$="
              " THEN GO SUB 3000
 140 GO TO 50
```

25

```
 500 PRINT AT 10,12; FLASH 1;"GA
ME OVER"
 501 PRINT AT 0,0; PAPER 5; INK
0;"SCORE ";s,"MISSILES ";mis;"  "
 510 PRINT AT 12,10;"You scored
";s
 520 IF s>hi THEN LET hi=s
 525 PRINT '' TAB 4;"Highest scor
e today ";hi
 530 INPUT "PRESS ENTER TO PLAY
AGAIN "; LINE a$: GO TO 30
1000 LET b=h+2
1010 FOR f=19 TO 4 STEP -1
1012 PRINT AT f,b;"A"
1019 BEEP .001,-(f-30)
1020 PRINT AT 5,0;a$''b$
1030 LET h=h+(INKEY$="8" AND h<3
0)-(INKEY$="5" AND h>0)
1040 PRINT AT 20,h; INK 6;"    "
1050 LET b$=b$(2 TO )+b$(1)
1060 LET a$=a$(LEN a$)+a$( TO (L
EN a$)-1)
1070 IF f=5 THEN IF a$(b)<>" " T
HEN GO TO 4000
1080 IF f=7 THEN IF b$(b)<>" " T
HEN GO TO 5000
1090 PRINT AT f,b;"  "
1100 NEXT f: RETURN
2000 PRINT AT 10,7; FLASH 1;"BON
US 1000 POINTS"
2010 LET b$="                    "
2011 LET s=s+1000
2015 BEEP .1,20: BEEP .2,15
2020 FOR p=1 TO 150: NEXT p
2040 PRINT AT 10,7;"
     ": RETURN
3000 PRINT AT 10,7; FLASH 1;"BON
US 2000 POINTS"
3010 LET a$="                    "
3011 LET s=s+2000
3015 BEEP .1,20: BEEP .2,15
3020 FOR p=1 TO 150: NEXT p
3030 PRINT AT 10,7;"
     ": RETURN
4000 LET a$(b-4 TO b+4)="
 "
4010 LET s=s+20
4011 BEEP .05,-5
4020 RETURN
5000 LET b$(b-4 TO b+4)="
 "
5010 LET s=s+10
```

26

```
5011 BEEP .05,-5
5020 RETURN
7000 BORDER 0: PAPER 1: INK 4: C
LS
7010 FOR a=0 TO 3: PRINT PAPER 5
; "     ";: NEXT a
7020 RETURN
8000 LET a$="�current graphic"
8010 LET b$="▼current graphic"
8020 LET h=15
8022 LET s=0
8030 RETURN
8900 REM *********************
8910 REM
8920 REM          Graphics
8930 REM
8940 REM     ▃▃▃      -    abc
8950 REM
8960 REM     ▼▼▼      -    defg
8970 REM
8980 REM      *       -    h
8990 REM
8999 REM *********************
9000 FOR a=USR "a" TO USR "h"+7
9010 READ user: POKE a,user
9020 NEXT a: RETURN
9030 DATA 0,0,0,127,255,255,255,
255
9040 DATA 0,24,60,255,255,255,25
5,255
9050 DATA 0,0,0,254,255,255,255,
255
9060 DATA 0,96,248,252,127,63,15
,7
9070 DATA 1,15,31,63,255,252,240
,192
9080 DATA 128,240,248,255,255,63
,31,7
9090 DATA 2,15,31,255,255,252,24
8,192
9100 DATA 24,60,60,24,60,36,0,0
```

27

SPIDER 'N' FLY

You are a very hungry spider hanging from a thread to the left of the screen, and the six rather fat flies that come into view are your main target. You have 99 seconds to eat as many flies as you can. Use key 6 to go up and 7 to go down.

```
 Score 8_____Time left 43
```

```
   10 REM Spider 'n fly
   20 LET hi=0: GO SUB 9000
   30 GO SUB 8000
   40 PRINT AT 0,0;"Score ";sc
   50 PRINT AT v,0;"  "
   60 LET v=v+(INKEY$="6" AND v<2
1)-(INKEY$="7" AND v>2)
   70 IF SCREEN$ (v,2)<>" " THEN
GO SUB 1000
   80 PRINT AT v-1,0;"|"
   90 PRINT AT v,0; INK 6;"#"
  100 FOR a=1 TO 5
  110 LET f(a)=f(a)-INT (RND*2):
IF f(a)<1 THEN PRINT AT a+3,1;"
 ": LET f(a)=28
  120 PRINT AT a+3,f(a); INK 4;"#
 "
  130 NEXT a
  140 PRINT AT 0,19;"Time left ";
INT time;" ": LET time=time-.5:
IF time<0 THEN GO TO 2000
  150 GO TO 50
  990 STOP
 1000 LET sc=sc+2
 1010 PRINT AT v,2;"   "
 1020 LET f(v/3)=28
 1030 PRINT AT 0,0; INK 7;"Score
";sc
 1040 RETURN
 2000 PRINT AT 5,9;"GAME OVER!"
 2010 PRINT ''TAB 6;"You scored "
;sc
```

29

```
2020 IF sc>hi THEN LET hi=sc
2030 PRINT ''"     highest score t
oday ";hi
2040 INPUT "Press "; FLASH 1;"EN
TER"; FLASH 0;" to play again ";
 LINE a$: GO TO 30
8000 BORDER 1: PAPER 1: INK 7: C
LS
8010 LET v=10
8020 DIM f(6)
8030 FOR a=1 TO 6: LET f(a)=28:
NEXT a
8040 LET sc=0
8050 RANDOMIZE
8060 FOR a=1 TO v-1: PRINT AT a,
0;"|": NEXT a
8070 PLOT 0,168: DRAW 255,0
8080 LET time=99
8090 RETURN
8991 REM
8992 REM          Graphics
8993 REM
8994 REM      ♣     graphics c
8995 REM      ♣♣    graphics ab
8996 REM
8997 REM      ☞    graphics de
8998 REM
8999 REM  *************************
9000 FOR a=USR "a" TO USR "a"+7
9010 READ user: POKE a,user
9020 NEXT a: RETURN
9030 DATA 60,126,255,255,127,127
,149,148
9040 DATA 0,108,248,220,252,248,
96,0
9050 DATA 16,16,16,16,16,16,16,1
6
9060 DATA 0,17,63,94,111,23,45,0
9070 DATA 0,252,2,2,252,224,0,0
```

30

ASCOT

In this program you can own a racehorse without the inconvenience of feeding it or mucking out the stable. You are given a racehorse and £50, and a chance to make a fortune on the track with that £50.

You can play the game with up to four friends; the winner is the person who finishes with the most money. To win money you place a bet on the horse of your choice, (you may only bet on one horse which you own for the five races), and the odds are displayed before each race. If you run out of money, but your horse wins a race, then you will be given a bonus amount so that you may continue play in the next race.

Race number 1

The odds on Red Gin
to win are 1:1

The odds on Sumley Gilds
to win are 1:1

The odds on Sparkle
to win are 5:1

The odds on Danny Boy
to win are 8:1

The odds on Shergart
to win are 3:1

Horse:- Red Gin

Owner:- Peter

You have £50

```
The winner is Danny Boy
Owned by Micheal

who wins 200




Horse:- Shergart

Owner:- Bill

You have £0

You have no money so you cannot
place a bet
```

```
   10 REM Ascot
   20 GO SUB 9000: REM UDG's
   30 GO SUB 8000
   40 FOR r=1 TO 5
   50 CLS
   60 PRINT AT 0,0;"Race number "
;r
   70 DIM d(p)
   80 FOR a=1 TO p: LET d(a)=INT
(RND*10)+1
   90 PRINT ''"The odds on ";h$(a)
  100 PRINT "to win are ";d(a);":
1"
  110 NEXT a
  120 GO SUB 5000
  130 PRINT AT 0,0;#1;"  Press an
y key to continue"
  140 PAUSE 0
  150 CLS : CIRCLE INK 2;240,165,
10: PLOT 240,155: DRAW INK 2;0,-
140: FOR a=1 TO p: PRINT AT a*3+
3,31;a: NEXT a
  155 DIM c(p)
  160 FOR a=1 TO p
  170 PRINT AT a*3+2,c(a);a$;AT a
*3+3,c(a);b$;AT a*3+4,c(a);c$
  180 LET c(a)=c(a)+(1/d(a)+INT (
RND*2))
  185 IF c(a)>25 THEN GO TO 250
  190 NEXT a
  200 FOR a=1 TO p: BEEP .008,c(a
)
```

33

```
 210 PRINT AT a*3+2,c(a);a$;AT a
*3+3,c(a);d$;AT a*3+4,c(a);e$
 220 LET c(a)=c(a)+(1/d(a)+INT (
RND*2))
 225 IF c(a)>25 THEN GO TO 250
 230 NEXT a
 240 GO TO 160
 250 LET w$=h$(a)
 260 PAUSE 100: CLS
 270 PRINT "The winner is ";w$
 280 PRINT "Owned by ";n$(a)
 290 LET ws=d(a)*s(a)
 300 PRINT "who wins ";ws. LET
m(a)=m(a)+ws+s(a)
 310 FOR z=1 TO 50: BEEP .008,z:
 BEEP .008,-z: NEXT z
 320 NEXT r
 330 CLS
 340 LET tot=0: PRINT "At the en
d of the game "
 350 FOR a=1 TO p
 360 PRINT n$(a);" has ";m(a)
 370 IF m(a)>tot THEN LET tot=m(
a): LET win=a
 380 NEXT a
 390 PRINT "So the winner is ";
n$(win)
 400 PRINT "on ";h$(win)
 410 PRINT "With £";m(win)
 420 INPUT "Press enter for anot
her game "; LINE z$: GO TO 30
 990 STOP
5000 FOR z=1 TO 50: BEEP .002*p,
z: BEEP .008,-z: NEXT z
5010 FOR a=1 TO p
5020 CLS
5030 PRINT "Horse:- ";h$(a)
5040 PRINT "Owner:- ";n$(a)
5050 PRINT "You have £";m(a)
5055 IF m(a)<1 THEN PRINT "You
have no money so you cannot plac
e a bet": PAUSE 150: NEXT a: RET
URN
5060 INPUT "How much will you be
t on the    next race £";s(a): I
F s(a)>m(a) THEN GO TO 5060
5070 LET m(a)=m(a)-s(a)
5080 NEXT a
5090 RETURN
8000 BORDER 0: PAPER 0: INK 7: C
LS : BEEP .1,10: BEEP .2,15
```

```
8010 LET a$="    <graphic>  ": REM abcd
8020 LET b$="    <graphic>  ": REM efgh
8030 LET c$="    <graphic>  ": REM ijkl
8040 LET d$="    <graphic>  ": REM emno
8050 LET e$="    <graphic>  ": REM ipq
8060 PRINT AT 1,12;"ASCOT"
8070 INPUT "How many players (Ma
x 5)"; LINE p$: IF p$<"1" OR p$>
"5" THEN GO TO 8070
8080 LET p=VAL p$: DIM s(p): DIM
 m(p): DIM n$(p,10): DIM h$(p,15
)
8090 FOR a=1 TO p
8100 PRINT AT 5,3;"Type in name
of player #";a
8110 INPUT "Max 10 letters "; LI
NE n$(a)
8120 LET m(a)=50: NEXT a
8125 CLS
8130 RESTORE 9200: FOR a=1 TO p
8140 READ h$(a): PRINT n$(a);" n
ow owns "'h$(a)''
8150 NEXT a
8160 PRINT AT 0,0;#1;"    Press a
ny key to continue": PAUSE 0
8990 RETURN
9000 FOR a=USR "a" TO USR "q"+7
9010 READ user: POKE a,user
9020 NEXT a: RETURN
9030 DATA 0,0,0,0,0,0,0,3
9040 DATA 0,0,0,0,0,1,113,207
9050 DATA 0,28,18,42,87,132,15,2
38
9060 DATA 0,0,16,248,60,124,199,
131
9070 DATA 5,13,13,9,9,9,9,0
9080 DATA 9,16,0,144,157,178,192
,192
9090 DATA 221,209,33,1,194,242,1
1,10
9100 DATA 128,0,0,0,0,0,0,128
9110 DATA 3,2,2,2,2,1,0,0
9120 DATA 192,192,96,32,16,32,0,
0
9130 DATA 13,28,25,19,18,8,0,0
9140 DATA 128,128,128,0,0,0,0,0
9150 DATA 16,0,16,144,177,167,64
,128
9160 DATA 69,1,1,1,194,246,20,20
9170 DATA 128,0,0,0,0,0,0,0
9180 DATA 128,128,128,128,128,64
,0,0
9190 DATA 28,28,24,24,20,12,10,0
9200 DATA "Red Gin","Sumley Bird
s","Sparkle","Danny Boy","Sherga
rt"
```

35

MUNCHIE MAN

This game is probably the highlight of this collection, a version of that unmentionable arcade game. It differs, however, in two main ways, although otherwise it is basically the same:

1. There is only one ghost.
2. When you eat the power pulls in the corners you get bonus points, not the chance to eat the ghost.

You use the cursor keys to control your movement.

Program Note
The graphics in lines 7010 and 7020 are obtained by swapping between Inv. video and True video, to get an inverse full stop and a true video underline (symbol shift Ø).

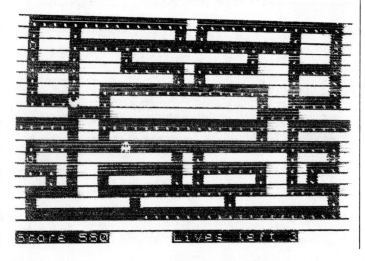

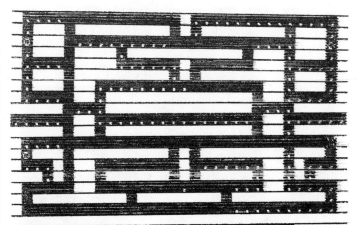

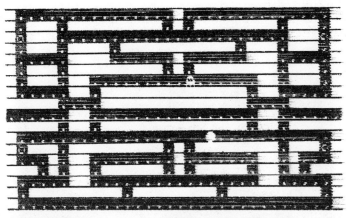

```
 10 REM Munchie Man
 20 LET hi=0: GO SUB 9000
 30 GO SUB 8000
 40 LET v=12: LET h=16: GO SUB
7000: INVERSE 1: PRINT AT 20,15;
"Lives left ";lives
```

```
   45 PRINT AT v,h; INVERSE 1;m$
   50 LET a$=INKEY$: IF a$<"5" OR
a$>"8" THEN GO TO 80
   60 IF a$<>"" THEN LET c1=VAL a
$
   70 LET m$=("♥" AND c1=7)+("♣"
AND c1=8)+("♠" AND c1=6)+("♦" AN
D c1=5)
   80 PRINT AT v,h;" "
   85 IF h<1 THEN LET h=30
   86 IF h>30 THEN LET h=0
   90 LET v1=v: LET h1=h
  100 LET v=v+(c1=6)-(c1=7)
  110 LET h=h+(c1=8)-(c1=5)
  120 IF SCREEN$ (v,h)="_" THEN L
ET v=v1: LET h=h1: PRINT AT v,h;
m$: GO TO 150
  130 IF SCREEN$ (v,h)="." THEN L
ET sc=sc+10: BEEP .008,10: LET c
ount=count+1
  135 IF SCREEN$ (v,h)="o" THEN G
O SUB 6000
  140 IF SCREEN$ (v,h)="" THEN GO
 TO 5000
  145 PRINT AT v,h;"●";AT 20,0;"S
core ";sc
  150 PRINT AT z,x;" "
  160 LET z1=z: LET x1=x
  170 LET z=z+(m1=6)-(m1=7): LET
x=x+(m1=8)-(m1=5)
  180 IF SCREEN$ (z,x)="_" THEN L
ET m1=INT (RND*4)+5: LET z=z1: L
ET x=x1: GO TO 160
  185 PRINT AT v,h;m$
  190 IF SCREEN$ (z,x)="." THEN P
RINT AT z1,x1;"."
  195 IF SCREEN$ (z,x)="o" THEN P
RINT AT z1,x1;"o"
  200 IF SCREEN$ (z,x)="" THEN GO
 TO 5000
  210 PRINT AT z,x; PAPER 4;"♠"
  230 IF lives<1 THEN GO TO 2000
  240 IF count=tot THEN LET count
=0: GO TO 40
  250 GO TO 50
  990 STOP
 2000 CLS
 2010 INVERSE 0: PRINT ''TAB 5;"G
AME OVER"
 2020 PRINT ''"           You scor
ed ";sc
 2030 IF sc>hi THEN LET hi=sc
 2040 PRINT ''"     Highest score t
oday ";hi
 2050 INPUT "Press enter to play
again "; LINE a$: GO TO 30
```

```
5000  INVERSE 1
5005  PRINT AT z,x;"."
5010  PRINT AT v,h;"●"
5020  BEEP .3,15
5030  PRINT AT v,h;"◡"
5040  BEEP .3,11
5050  PRINT AT v,h;"●"
5060  BEEP .3,7
5070  PRINT AT v,h;"▲"
5080  BEEP .3,3
5090  PRINT AT v,h;"✕"
5100  BEEP .3,0
5110  PRINT AT v,h;" "
5120  BEEP .5,-5
5130  LET count=0: LET v=12: LET
      h=16: LET lives=lives-1
5140  INVERSE 0: GO TO 40
6000  BEEP .008,15: BEEP .005,-15
      : LET sc=sc+INT (RND*100)+200
6010  RETURN
7000  PAPER 0: CLS : INK 0: PAPER
      6: BORDER 0
7010  PRINT "
```

```
7020  PRINT "
```

```
7030  INK 0
7040  PAPER 6
7100  RETURN
8000  LET m$="●"
8020  LET ci=6: LET mi=5
8030  LET sc=0
8040  LET z=7: LET x=15
8050  LET lives=3
8060  LET count=0
8070  LET tot=266
8990  RETURN
```

39

```
9000 FOR a=USR "a" TO USR "i"+7
9010 READ user: POKE a,user
9020 NEXT a: RETURN
9030 DATA 60,126,255,255,255,255
,126,60
9040 DATA 0,66,195,231,255,255,1
26,60
9050 DATA 60,126,248,240,240,248
,126,60
9060 DATA 60,126,255,255,231,195
,66,0
9070 DATA 60,126,31,15,15,31,126
,60
9080 DATA 0,0,126,255,255,255,12
6,60
9090 DATA 0,0,0,0,16,24,60,60
9100 DATA 129,66,36,0,0,36,66,12
9
9110 DATA 28,62,42,107,127,127,1
09,73
9980 REM a b c d e f g h i
9990 REM ● ● ● ● ● ● ● ● ●
```

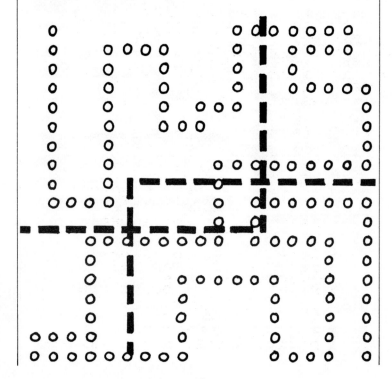

40

TRACK TRAP

In this game you and the computer move around the screen, leaving a trail and competing for space. If you run into the computer's track or the side of the screen, or if you double back on yourself, then the computer gains a point. The computer is not unbeatable however, and with practice you should take great pleasure in outwitting it. Use the cursor keys to control your movements.

```
  10 REM Track trap
  20 LET hi=0
  30 GO SUB 8000
  40 LET a$=INKEY$
  50 IF a$)"3" OR a$<"5" THEN GO
TO 70
  60 LET m=VAL a$: LET j=0
  70 LET h1=h1+(m=6)-(m=7)
  80 LET h2=h2+(m=8)-(m=5)
  90 LET b$=SCREEN$ (h1,h2)
 100 BEEP .005,10
 110 IF b$="_" THEN GO SUB 2000
 120 LET j=1: PRINT AT h1,h2; IN
VERSE 1;" "
 130 PRINT AT h1,h2; INVERSE 1;
INK 6;" "
 140 LET u=0
 150 IF u=5 THEN GO SUB 1000
 160 LET c3=c1: LET c4=c2
 170 LET c1=c1+(n=6)-(n=7)
 180 LET c2=c2+(n=8)-(n=5)
 190 LET c$=SCREEN$ (c1,c2)
 200 IF c$="_" THEN LET n=u+5: L
ET c1=c3: LET c2=c4: LET u=u+1:
GO TO 150
 220 PRINT AT c1,c2; INVERSE 1;"
 "
 240 GO TO 40
1000 PRINT AT c1,c2; FLASH 1;"_"
1010 LET hs=hs+1: FOR p=1 TO 38:
 BEEP .008,p: NEXT p
1020 PRINT AT 0,0;"SCORE COMP ";
cs;"      HUMAN ";hs
1030 PRINT INVERSE 1;"_____
 "
1040 FOR l=1 TO 19
1050 PRINT INVERSE 1;"_"; INVERS
E 0;"
```

```
      "; INVERSE 1;"_"
1060 NEXT l
1070 PRINT INVERSE 1;"_____
                                "
1080 LET c1=10: LET c2=10
1090 LET h1=10: LET h2=20
1100 IF hs=10 THEN GO TO 3000
1110 RETURN
2000 PRINT AT h1,h2; FLASH 1;"▔▔"
2010 LET cs=cs+1: FOR p=1 TO 30:
 BEEP .008,p: NEXT p
2020 PRINT AT 0,0;"SCORE COMP ";
cs;"       HUMAN ";hs
2030 PRINT INVERSE 1;"_____
                                "
2040 FOR l=1 TO 19
2050 PRINT INVERSE 1;"_"; INVERS
E 0;"
   "; INVERSE 1;"_"
2060 NEXT l
2070 PRINT INVERSE 1;"_____
                                "
2080 LET c1=10: LET c2=10
2090 LET h1=10: LET h2=20
2100 IF cs=10 THEN GO TO 3000
2110 RETURN
3000 PRINT AT 5,8;("COMPUTER " A
ND cs>hs)+("HUMAN " AND hs>cs);"
 WINS!!"
3010 INPUT "Press enter to play
again "; LINE a$
8000 LET j=1: LET c1=10: LET c2=
10
8010 LET h1=10: LET h2=20
8020 LET hs=0: LET cs=0
8030 BORDER 0: PAPER INT (RND*6)
: INK 9: CLS
8040 PRINT "SCORE ";
8050 PRINT "COMP 00   HUMAN 00"
8060 PRINT INVERSE 1;"_____
                                "
8070 FOR l=1 TO 19
8080 PRINT INVERSE 1;"_";TAB 31;
 INVERSE 1;"_"
8090 NEXT l
8100 PRINT INVERSE 1;"_____
                                "
8110 LET m=5: LET n=8: RETURN
```

42

PONTOON

This is a slightly simplified version of the popular card game, and just as compelling to play. The object of the game is to get as close as possible to a score of 21 without exceeding it.

It is your turn first. The computer displays your first two cards and you then have to decide whether to accept another card — 'Twist' — or to stay as you are — 'Stick'. You have to make the decision perhaps two, three or more times. If your total exceeds 21 the computer announces 'You Are Bust' and you lose £10 (the charge per game). Once you have decided to 'Stick' with a score less than 21 the computer deals its own hand (this is not displayed). The computer will then either 'Bust' or 'Stick' before reporting which of you was the winner.

An ace can only be worth one, and five card tricks do not count. When you have had enough of the game, break the program when the computer is dealing the cards.

```
D - Deal
T - twist
S - Stick
```

Cash 90

BUST

I win that game!

    T - twist

    S - Stick

Cash 50

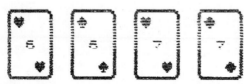

I have 21

You have 19

PONTOON!

```
  10 REM Pontoon
  20 GO SUB 9000
  30 LET money=50
  40 GO SUB 7000
  50 LET c1=INT (RND*10)+1
  60 LET c2=INT (RND*10)+1
  70 PRINT AT 11,2;"┌───────┐"
  80 LET b$=CHR$ (144+(INT (RND*
4)))
  90 PRINT AT 12,2;"│";b$;"    │"
 100 PRINT AT 13,2;"│       │"
 110 PRINT AT 14,2;"│   ";(CHR$ 6
AND c1=10);c1;"   │"
 120 PRINT AT 15,2;"│       │"
 130 PRINT AT 16,2;"│    ";b$;"│"
 140 PRINT AT 17,2;"└───────┘"
 150 LET b$=CHR$ (144+(INT (RND*
4)))
 160 PRINT AT 11,8;"┌───────┐"
 170 PRINT AT 12,8;"│";b$;"    │"
 180 PRINT AT 13,8;"│       │"
 190 PRINT AT 14,8;"│   ";(CHR$ 6
AND c2=10);c2;"   │"
 200 PRINT AT 15,8;"│       │"
 210 PRINT AT 16,8;"│    ";b$;"│"
 220 PRINT AT 17,8;"└───────┘"
```

```
  225 LET tot=c1+c2: LET c3=INT (
RND*10)+1
  230 PRINT
  235 PRINT AT 5,5;"T - twist"
  240 PRINT AT 7,5;"S - stick"
  240 IF INKEY$="t" OR INKEY$="s"
THEN GO TO 250
  245 GO TO 240
  250 IF INKEY$="s" THEN GO TO 10
00
  260 LET tot=tot+c3
  270 LET b$=CHR$ (144+(INT (RND*
4)))
  275 IF p>26 THEN LET p=2: CLS
  280 PRINT AT 11,p;"
  290 PRINT AT 12,p;" ";b$;"   "
  300 PRINT AT 13,p;"          "
  310 PRINT AT 14,p;"   ";(CHR$ 8
AND c3=10);c3;"
  320 PRINT AT 15,p;"
  330 PRINT AT 16,p;"   ";b$;"
  340 PRINT AT 17,p;"
  350 IF tot>21 THEN PRINT AT 1,1
;"BUST": GO TO 2000
  360 LET p=p+6
  365 LET c3=INT (RND*10)+1
  370 GO TO 240
  990 STOP
 1000 LET cs=INT (RND*13)+10
 1010 CLS
 1020 PRINT '"I have ";cs''"You h
ave ";tot'
 1030 IF cs>21 THEN PRINT "I have
 bust, You win ": GO TO 1070
 1040 IF cs=21 THEN PRINT "PONTOO
N!": GO TO 1070
 1050 IF cs>=tot THEN PRINT "I wi
n": GO TO 1070
 1060 PRINT "You win £50!": LET m
oney=money+50
 1070 FOR k=1 TO 60: BEEP .008,k:
 BEEP .008,-k: NEXT k: GO TO 40
 2000 PRINT '"I win that game!"
 2010 GO TO 1070
 3000 CLS
 3010 PRINT AT 10,7;"You're out o
f money"
 3020 INPUT "Press enter to play
again "; LINE a$: RUN
 7000 BORDER 0: PAPER 4: INK 4: C
LS
 7005 LET p=14: LET money=money-1
0: IF money<0 THEN GO TO 3000
 7010 PRINT AT 1,24; INK 1;"
"
 7020 FOR a=1 TO 6
 7030 PRINT TAB 24; INK 1;"
```

45

```
7040 NEXT a
7050 PRINT TAB 24; INK 1;"◣___◢"
;AT 9,23;"Cash ";money
7060 PRINT AT 3,5;"D - Deal"
7070 IF INKEY$<>"d" THEN GO TO 7
070
7080 RETURN
7990 RETURN
9000 FOR a=USR "a" TO USR "k"+7
9010 READ user: POKE a,user
9020 NEXT a: RETURN
9030 DATA 24,60,126,255,255,126,
60,24
9040 DATA 24,60,90,255,255,90,24
,60
9050 DATA 16,56,124,254,254,84,1
6,56
9060 DATA 68,238,254,254,254,124
,56,16
9070 DATA 204,204,51,51,204,204,
51,51
9080 DATA 0,0,0,7,15,12,24,24
9090 DATA 0,0,0,192,240,48,24,24
9100 DATA 24,24,12,15,7,0,0,0
9110 DATA 24,24,48,240,192,0,0,0
9120 DATA 0,0,0,255,255,0,0,0
9130 DATA 24,24,24,24,24,24,24,2
4
9990 REM a b c d e f g h i j k
9991 REM ♠ ♣ ♣ ♥ ▓ , ╲ ╰ ╱ ─ ┆
```

BREAKOUT

This is a version of the old favourite. The object of the game is to score points by knocking bricks out of a wall, using a ball which you keep in play by bouncing it back at the wall off your bat. You have ten balls to play with. The game ends when the tenth ball goes out of play. Key 5 moves your bat left and key 8 moves it right. There is also a choice of speeds, input 1 for fast, anything above 10 for slow.

```
   10 REM Breakout
   20 GO SUB 9000
   30 GO SUB 8000
   35 GO SUB 7000
   40 PRINT AT 20,v;"  _____  "
   50 LET v=v+2*(INKEY$="8" AND v
<27)-2*(INKEY$="5" AND v>0): IF
INKEY$="5" AND v<0 THEN PRINT AT
 20,1;"_____  "
   55 PRINT AT 0,0;"SCORE ";sc: F
OR a=1 TO s: NEXT a
   60 PRINT AT e,f;"  "
   70 LET e=e+c: IF e<2 THEN LET
c=-c: BEEP .008,20
   80 LET f=f+d: IF f<1 OR f>50 T
HEN LET d=-d: BEEP .008,10
   90 IF SCREEN$ (e,f)="_" THEN L
ET sc=sc+1: LET c=-c: BEEP .008,
15
   95 IF SCREEN$ (e,f)="_" THEN L
ET count=count+1: IF count=(52*5
) THEN LET count=0: LET s=s-(s>1
): GO TO 35
  100 IF SCREEN$ (e,f)="" THEN LE
T c=-c: BEEP .008,15
  110 PRINT AT e,f; INK 6;"●": IF
 e>20 THEN LET b=b+1: GO SUB 100
0
  115 IF b=10 THEN GO TO 2000
  130 GO TO 40
  990 STOP
 1000 PRINT AT e,f;"  "
 1010 LET e=20: LET f=INT (RND*16
)+10: LET c=-1
 1020 PRINT AT 0,25;"BALL ";b
 1030 RETURN
 2000 PRINT AT 10,12;"GAME OVER"
 2010 PRINT ''"          You Sco
red ";sc
 2020 INPUT "Press Enter to play
again "; LINE a$: GO TO 30
 7000 PRINT AT 0,0;"SCORE 0";AT 0
,25;"BALL 1": FOR a=1 TO 3
 7010 PRINT ' INK a+2; INVERSE 1;
"
"
 7020 NEXT a
 7030 RETURN
 8000 BORDER 0: PAPER 1: INK 7: C
LS
 8010 LET v=15
 8020 LET c=-1: LET d=1
 8030 LET sc=0
 8040 LET e=20: LET f=INT (RND*15
)+10
```

48

```
8050 LET b=1
8060 INPUT "What speed (1-Fast 2
0-Extra slow)";s
8070 LET count=0
8990 RETURN
9000 FOR a=USR "a" TO USR "b"+7
9010 READ user: POKE a,user
9020 NEXT a: RETURN
9030 DATA 60,126,255,255,255,255
,126,60
9040 DATA 0,0,0,0,0,0,255,255
9990 REM a b
9991 REM ● _
```

EXCALIBUR AGAINST THE ENEMY

This game is played on a seven by seven grid. You are commanding the SS Excalibur and you have to defend yourself against a number of alien spaceships. If the alien ships box you in so that you cannot move they win. To win you have to capture at least 17 enemy ships by jumping over them — before 50 moves are up. You can move up and down and to the left and right but not diagonally. You jump to the next but one position in the direction you have chosen.

To make your move you enter the number of the square you want to move into. Type the appropriate number from the side column, followed by the number across as one number — that is, without any spaces or commas in between. Your computer will notice immediately if you make an illegal move. You can move into any sector that contains stars but not one with an enemy ship or square in it.

```
 10 REM Excalibur Against the
    enemy
 20 RANDOMIZE : GO SUB 9000
 30 GO SUB 600
 40 GO SUB 80
 50 GO SUB 380
 60 GO SUB 80
 70 GO TO 50
 80 REM -Computer Moves-
 90 LET y=0: LET p=p+1
100 LET k=INT (RND*63)+13
110 LET y=y+1
120 IF h(k)<>144 THEN GO TO 100
```

```
  130 LET  j=1
  140 IF  h(k+z(j))=146 THEN  GO TO
190
  150 LET  j=j+1
  160 IF  j<3 THEN  GO TO 140
  170 IF  y<100 THEN  GO TO 100
  180 PRINT "Excalibur wins!!
 STOP
  190 LET  h(k)=146: LET  h(k+z(j))
=144
  200 RETURN
  210 REM -Accept player move-
  220 PRINT
  230 REM Player enters 99 for q
if no move
  240 LET  q=qm
  250 REM Input at top of screen-
  260 INPUT AT 4,0;AT 0,0;"Excali
bur moves to ";l
  270 IF  l=99 THEN  GO TO 750
  280 REM -Mugtraps-
  290 LET  r=ABS  (l-q)
  300 IF  h(q)<>69 OR h(l)<>146 TH
EN PRINT "Illegal move": GO TO 2
30
  310 IF  r=9 OR r=18 OR r=18 OR r
=22 THEN PRINT "Diagonal moves a
re illegal.": GO TO 230
  330 LET  h(q)=146: LET  h(l)=69
  340 IF  r=20 OR r=2 THEN LET h((
l+q)/2)=146: LET  s=s+1
  350 LET  qm=l
  360 RETURN
  370 REM -Print board-
  380 PRINT
  390 PRINT : PRINT TAB 3;"Move n
umber ";P
  400 IF  k=0 OR k+z(j)=10 OR k=k+
z(j) THEN  GO TO 420
  410 PRINT
  420 PRINT 50-p;" Moves Left ":
PRINT
  430 PRINT TAB 4;"1234567"
  440 FOR  j=70 TO 10 STEP  -10
  450 LET  a=h(j+1): LET  b=h(j+2)
: LET  c=h(j+3): LET  d=h(j+4): LE
T e=h(j+5): LET  f=h(j+6): LET  g=
h(j+7)
  470 PRINT TAB 3;j/10;
  480 PRINT CHR$  (a);CHR$  (b);CH
R$  (c);CHR$  (d);CHR$  (e);CHR$ (f
);CHR$  (g);j/10
  490 NEXT  j
  500 PRINT TAB 4;"1234567"
  510 PRINT
```

51

```
 520 IF p=50 THEN GO TO 740
 530 PRINT " Enemy tally:";17-s;
" Ships to go!"
 540 IF s=17 THEN GO TO 180
 550 GO SUB 210
 560 IF k=0 THEN GO TO 580
 570 RETURN
 580 FOR j=1 TO 750: NEXT j
 590 RETURN
 600 BORDER 0: PAPER 0: INK 6: B
RIGHT 1: CLS
 610 DIM h(87): DIM z(5): LET k=
0: LET s=0: LET p=0
 620 RESTORE 630: FOR j=1 TO 3:
READ q: LET z(j)=q: NEXT j
 630 DATA 10,1,-1
 640 LET j=1: LET l=100
 650 FOR a=1 TO 87: LET h(a)=145
 660 IF a>72 AND a<76 OR a>62 AN
D a<66 OR a>51 AND a<57 OR a>41
AND a<47 THEN LET h(a)=146
 680 IF a=51 OR a=41 OR a=57 OR
a=47 THEN LET h(a)=144
 690 IF a>30 AND a<38 OR a>22 AN
D a<26 OR a>12 AND a<16 THEN LET
h(a)=144
 700 NEXT a
 710 LET h(44)=69
 720 LET qm=44
 730 RETURN
 740 PRINT " Time is up!"
 750 PRINT "Enemy Tally is ";s
 760 PRINT
 770 INPUT AT 20,0;AT 0,0;"Anoth
er game (y or n)",w$
 780 IF w$="y" THEN GO TO 30
 790 PRINT
 800 PRINT "I'm glad you know wh
en you're    beaten,"
 810 PRINT
 820 PRINT ,"Excalibur"
 830 STOP
9000 RESTORE 9000: FOR a=USR "a"
TO USR "c"+7
9010 READ user: POKE a,user
9020 NEXT a: RETURN
9030 DATA 24,24,60,90,153,189,19
5,129
9040 DATA 255,129,129,129,129,12
9,129,255
9050 DATA 0,0,1,0,4,0,0,16
```

52

LEAKY ROOF

The roof is leaking and you only have one bucket. Catch the drips in the bucket using key 5 to go left and key 8 to go right. The rain will last for thirty drips, so catch as many as you can and save yourself having to call in the builder.

```
  10 REM Leaky Roof
  20 GO SUB 9000: LET hi=0
  30 GO SUB 8000
  40 GO SUB 7000
  50 LET p=INT (RND*30)+1: LET d
=d+1: PRINT AT 0,25;"Drip ";d
  60 FOR l=6 TO 18
  70 PRINT AT 20,v; INK 6;"    "
;AT 21,v;"    "
  80 PRINT AT l,p; INK 5;"  ";AT
 l+1,p;"  ";AT l+2,p;"  "
  90 IF l+3=20 AND v+1=p+1 OR l+
3=20 AND v+2=p+1 OR l+3=20 AND v
+2=p THEN LET sc=sc+1: PRINT AT
0,0;"SCORE ";sc
 100 LET v=v+(INKEY$="8" AND v<2
8)-(INKEY$="5" AND v>0)
 110 NEXT l
 120 PRINT AT l,p;"   ";AT l+1,p;
"   "
 130 IF d=30 THEN GO TO 150
 140 GO TO 50
 150 PRINT AT 5,11;"GAME OVER"
 160 PRINT ,,,,"            You sc
ored ";sc
 170 IF sc>hi THEN LET hi=sc
 180 PRINT ,,"            Highest scor
e today ";hi
 190 INPUT "Press ENTER to play
again "; LINE a$: GO TO 30

7000 CLS
7010 PRINT "SCORE ";sc
7020 PRINT INK 2;"             "
7025 PRINT INK 2;"             "
7030 PRINT INK 2;"             "
```

```
7035 PRINT INK 2;"████████████
████████████"
7990 RETURN
8000 BORDER 0: PAPER 0: INK 7: C
LS : BRIGHT 0
8010 LET sc=0
8020 LET v=15
8030 LET d=0
8990 RETURN
9000 FOR a=USR "a" TO USR "j"+7
9010 READ user: POKE a,user
9020 NEXT a: RETURN
9030 DATA 255,255,255,255,255,25
5,0,0
9040 DATA 252,252,252,252,252,25
2,0,0
9050 DATA 0,0,0,0,0,1,3,7
9060 DATA 0,0,0,0,0,128,192,224
9070 DATA 7,7,15,15,15,7,7,3
9080 DATA 224,224,240,240,240,22
4,224,192
9090 DATA 0,0,127,63,95,111,119,
59
9100 DATA 0,0,254,254,253,251,25
1,246
9110 DATA 62,63,63,63,31,31,31,3
1
9120 DATA 14,254,254,254,252,252
,252,252
9130 REM a b c d e f g h i j
9140 REM ██ ▪▪ ▪▪ ██ ██ ██
```

TOUCHDOWN ON MARS

Can you land your space module in the landing patch?
The entrance is narrow and it takes a keen eye to land
safely. After the first landing you get another module
which descends faster than the first one, so beware —
make sure your aim is good, otherwise you might crash
and you could be stranded on Mars for ever. Use key 5 to
go left and key 8 to go right.

```
  10 REM Touchdown on Mars
  20 GO SUB 9000: LET hi=0
  30 GO SUB 8000
  40 GO SUB 7000
  50 PRINT AT v,h;"   ";AT v+1,h;
"  "
  60 LET v=v+(((sc/5)+1)/5): LET
h=h+(INKEY$="8" AND h<31)-(INKE
Y$="5" AND h>0)
  70 IF SCREEN$ (v+1,h)<>" " THE
N GO TO 1000
  80 PRINT AT v,h; INK 6;"▲";AT
v+1,h;"▼"
  90 IF v>20 THEN GO TO 2000
 100 PRINT AT 21,24;"SCORE ";sc
 110 LET t=t+.1
 120 PRINT AT 21,0;"TIME ";INT t
 150 GO TO 50
 990 STOP
1000 PRINT AT 2,5;"GAME OVER IN
";t;" SECONDS"
1010 PRINT AT v,h; FLASH 1; INK
6;"▲";AT v+1,h;"▼"
1020 FOR p=1 TO 100: NEXT p
1030 IF sc>hi THEN LET hi=sc
1040 PRINT AT 7,9;"You scored ";
sc
1050 PRINT AT 9,5;"Highest score
today ";hi
1060 INPUT "Press ENTER to play
again "; LINE a$: GO TO 30
2000 LET v=0: LET h=0: LET sc=sc
+1
2010 CLS
2020 GO TO 40
7000 LET b=INT (RND*16)+10: LET
b=b*8
7010 FOR a=0 TO b-10: PLOT a,0:
DRAW 0,(INT (RND*50)+50)
7020 NEXT a
7040 FOR a=b+10 TO 255: PLOT a,0
: DRAW 0,INT (RND*50)+50
7050 NEXT a
7990 RETURN
8000 BORDER 0: PAPER 0: INK 2: C
LS
8010 LET h=0: LET v=0
8020 LET t=0: LET sc=0
8990 RETURN
9000 FOR a=USR "a" TO USR "d"+7
9010 READ user: POKE a,user
9020 NEXT a: RETURN
9030 DATA 0,0,7,15,31,53,53,53
9040 DATA 0,0,224,240,248,172,17
2,172
```

```
9050 DATA 31,13,18,16,8,4,14,0
9060 DATA 246,176,72,8,16,32,112
,0
9070 REM a b c d
9080 REM
7000>LET b=INT (RND*16)+10: LET
b=b*8
7010 FOR a=0 TO b-10: PLOT a,0:
DRAW 0,(INT (RND*50)+50)
7020 NEXT a
7040 FOR a=b+10 TO 255: PLOT a,0
: DRAW 0,INT (RND*50)+50
7050 NEXT a
7990 RETURN
8000 BORDER 0: PAPER 0: INK 2: C
LS
8010 LET h=0: LET v=0
8020 LET t=0: LET sc=0
8990 RETURN
9000 FOR a=USR "a" TO USR "d"+7
9010 READ user: POKE a,user
9020 NEXT a: RETURN
```

ORCHARD THIEF

Collect as many apples as you can in the orchard before the farmer arrives and the game is over. You score three points for every apple that is eaten, and if you manage to eat all 50 apples in the 30 second time limit then you score bonus points.

```
   10 REM Orchard Thief
   20 GO SUB 9000: LET hi=0
   30 GO SUB 6000: GO SUB 7000
   40 PRINT AT v,h;" "
   45 LET v1=v: LET h1=h
   50 LET v=v+(INKEY$="6" AND v<2
0)-(INKEY$="7" AND v>1)
   60 LET h=h+(INKEY$="8" AND h<3
1)-(INKEY$="5" AND v>0)
   70 IF SCREEN$ (v,h)="_" THEN L
ET v=v1: LET h=h1: GO TO 45
   80 IF SCREEN$ (v,h)="" THEN LE
T sc=sc+3: LET co=co+1
   90 PRINT AT v,h; INK 6;"♣"
  100 LET ti=ti+.1: PRINT AT 0,0;
 PAPER 2;"SCORE ";sc,"TIME ";INT
 ti
  105 BEEP .006,co
  110 IF ti>30 THEN GO TO 1000
  120 IF co=50 THEN GO TO 2000
  130 GO TO 40
 1000 PRINT AT v,h; FLASH 1; INK
2;"♣"
 1010 PRINT AT 1,12; PAPER 1;"GAM
E OVER"
 1020 PRINT AT 5,7; PAPER 2;"YOU
RAN OUT OF TIME"
 1030 PRINT AT 12,10;"YOU SCORED
";sc
 1040 IF sc>hi THEN LET hi=sc
 1050 PRINT AT 20,6;"Highest scor
e today ";hi
 1060 INPUT "   Press enter to pla
y again   "; LINE a$: GO TO 30
 2000 PRINT AT v,h; FLASH 1; INK
6;"♣"
 2010 PRINT AT 2,10; PAPER 1;"GAM
E OVER"
 2020 PRINT AT 5,3; PAPER 2;"YOU
DID IT IN ";INT ti;" TIME UNITS"
 2030 PRINT AT 7,10; PAPER 4; FLA
SH 1;"BONUS ";INT (100-ti)*3
 2040 LET sc=sc+INT (100-ti)*3
 2050 GO TO 1030
 7040 PRINT AT 0,0; PAPER 2;"SCOR
E ";sc,"TIME ";ti,
 7050 PRINT INVERSE 1; INK 6;"___
                                "
 7060 FOR a=1 TO 18
 7070 PRINT INVERSE 1; INK 6;"_";
 INVERSE 0;TAB 31; INVERSE 1;"_";
 7080 NEXT a
 7090 PRINT INVERSE 1; INK 6;"___
                                "
 7095 FOR a=1 TO 50
```

59

```
7100 LET j=INT (RND*18)+2: LET k
=INT (RND*29)+2
7110 IF j=v AND k=h THEN GO TO 7
100
7115 IF SCREEN$ (j,k)="" THEN GO
TO 7100
7120 PRINT AT j,k; INK 4;"◆": NE
XT a
7130 RETURN
8000 BORDER 0. PAPER 0. INK 9: C
LS
8010 LET v=INT (RND*18)+2: LET h
=INT (RND*29)+2
8020 LET co=0: LET ti=0
8030 LET sc=0
8040 RETURN
9000 FOR a=USR "a" TO USR "b"+7
9010 READ user: POKE a,user
9020 NEXT a: RETURN
9030 DATA 12,24,62,127,127,127,1
27,62
9040 DATA 28,28,8,63,8,28,34,65
9050 REM a b
9060 REM ◆ ☘
```

CHARGE OF THE TEDDY

Teddy wants to get to the screen but unfortunately there are a number of laser blasters firing across his path. If you are able to avoid these, Teddy will be safe. You score three points for every Teddy safely home, and you start the game with five teddies. Use the cursor keys to control your movement.

```
  10 REM Charge of the Teddybear
  20 REM Peter Shaw
  30 REM Original idea by
         Steven Gunning
  40 GO SUB 9000: LET hi=0
  50 GO SUB 8000: GO SUB 7000
  60 PRINT AT v,h; OVER 1; PAPER
8; INK 6;"  ";AT v+1,h;"  "
  70 LET v=v+2*(INKEY$="6" AND v
<19)-2*(INKEY$="7" AND v>0)
  80 LET h=h+2*(INKEY$="8" AND h
<29)-2*(INKEY$="5" AND h>1)
  90 PRINT AT v,h; OVER 1; PAPER
8; INK 6;"  ";AT v+1,h;"  "
 100 GO SUB 1000
 110 IF v=0 THEN GO SUB 2000
 115 PRINT AT 21,0; PAPER 2;"SCO
RE ";sc;"TEDDIES LEFT ";td;
 120 BEEP .008,sc
 130 GO TO 60
 990 STOP
1000 LET r=INT (RND*6)+1
1010 PLOT 8,m(r): DRAW INK 8;240
,0
1020 LET p=(21-((m(r)-4)/8))
1030 IF v=p OR v=p-1 THEN GO TO
3000
1035 PLOT 8,m(r): DRAW INK 8;240
,0
1040 PLOT 8,m(r): DRAW OVER 1;24
0,0
1050 RETURN
2000 PRINT AT v,h; PAPER 8;"  ";
AT v+1,h;"  ";
2005 BEEP .1,20
2010 LET sc=sc+3
2020 LET v=18: LET h=15
2030 PRINT AT v,h; INK 6; PAPER
8; OVER 1;"  ";AT v+1,h;"  "
2040 RETURN
3000 PRINT AT v,h; INK 2; FLASH
1;"  ";AT v+1,h;"  "
3001 BEEP .5,-10
3005 LET td=td-1: IF td=-1 THEN
GO TO 4000
3010 PRINT AT v,h;"  ";AT v+1,h;
"  "
3020 LET v=18: LET h=15
3030 PRINT AT v,h; INK 6; PAPER
8; OVER 1;"  ";AT v+1,h;"  "
3040 GO TO 1035
4000 PRINT AT 2,12; PAPER 6;"GAM
E OVER"
4010 PRINT ''TAB 10; PAPER 1;"YO
```

```
U SCORED ";sc
4020 IF sc>hi THEN LET hi=sc
4030 PRINT AT 18,6; PAPER 6;"Hig
hest score today ";hi
4040 INPUT "Press "; PAPER 2;"EN
TER"; PAPER 0;" to play again ";
 LINE a$
4050 GO TO 50
4990 STOP
7000 CLS
7010 PRINT PAPER 1,,
7020 PLOT 0,14: DRAW 0,152
7030 PLOT 255,14: DRAW 0,152
7040 FOR a=2 TO 17 STEP 5
7050 PRINT AT a,0; "►";AT a,31; "◄
"
7060 NEXT a
7070 PRINT AT 20,0; PAPER 1,,
7080 PLOT 0,8: DRAW 255,0
7090 PRINT AT 21,0;"SCORE ";sc,"
TEDDIES LEFT ";td
7100 PRINT AT v,h; OVER 1; PAPER
 8; INK 6;"▓▓";AT v+1,h; "▓▓"
7990 RETURN
8000 BORDER 0: PAPER 0: INK 9: C
LS
8010 LET sc=0: DIM m(5): LET v=1
8: LET h=15
8020 RESTORE 9090: FOR a=1 TO 6
8030 READ m(a): NEXT a
8040 LET co=0
8050 LET td=5
8990 RETURN
9000 FOR a=USR "a" TO USR "f"+7
9010 READ user: POKE a,user
9020 NEXT a: RETURN
9030 DATA 0,56,127,127,127,125,5
6,29
9040 DATA 0,28,254,254,254,222,1
40,220
9050 DATA 31,31,31,31,30,15,7,3
9060 DATA 252,252,124,124,60,248
,240,224
9070 DATA 128,128,224,255,255,22
4,128,128
9080 DATA 1,1,7,255,255,7,1,1
9090 DATA 36,60,84,108,132,156
9998 REM ► ◄
9999 REM ▓▓
```

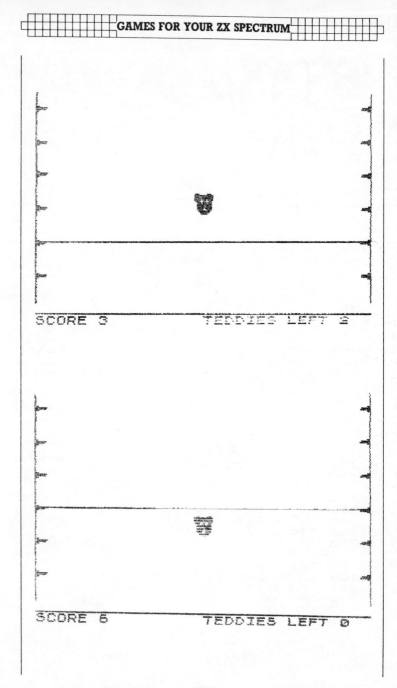

SCORE 3   TEDDIES LEFT 2

SCORE 6   TEDDIES LEFT 0

64

SNAKE IN THE TRIANGLES

You are a snake making your angular but winding way down the screen. A number of deadly poisonous blue triangles are rapidly coming towards you; you must avoid these at all costs since if you should hit one the game will be over. You automatically go left, so use key 8 to control your movement right.

```
  10 REM Snake in the Triangles
  20 GO SUB 9000: LET hi=0
  30 GO SUB 8000
  40 PRINT AT 9,h;" "
  50 LET h=h+2*(INKEY$="8" AND h
<29): IF h>0 THEN LET h=h-1
  54 IF SCREEN$ (10,h)="" THEN G
O TO 1000
  55 PRINT AT 9,h; INK 6;"♥";AT
10,h;"▓"
  60 PRINT AT 21,0;
  70 PRINT TAB INT (RND*31); INK
1;"▼"
  80 POKE 23692,255
  90 LET sc=sc+1: PRINT '
 100 GO TO 40
1000 PRINT AT 0,0; OVER 1; PAPER
 6; INK 2;v$(1)
1010 PRINT AT 1,10; FLASH 1;"GAM
E OVER"
1020 PRINT AT 5,7;"You scored ";
sc
1030 IF sc>hi THEN LET hi=sc
1040 PRINT AT 10,5;"Highest scor
e today ";hi
1050 INPUT "Press "; PAPER 1;"EN
TER"; PAPER 0;" to play again ";
 LINE a$: GO TO 30
1090 STOP
```

```
8000  BORDER 0: PAPER 0: INK 9: C
LS : LET v=10: LET h=15
8010  LET sc=0: RANDOMIZE
8020  DIM v$(1,704)
8090  RETURN
9000  FOR a=USR "a" TO USR "c"+7
9010  READ user: POKE a,user
9020  NEXT a: RETURN
9030  DATA 255,126,126,60,60,24,2
4,0
9040  DATA 0,99,119,127,62,28,0,0
9050  DATA 99,119,73,73,127,62,28
,0
```

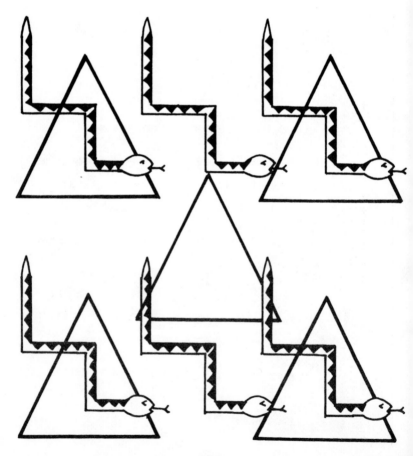

66

DEATH RACE

The idea of this game is to knock down as many pedestrians as possible and — as with the film of the same name — you score points for each pedestrian hit. When you hit your target a gravestone appears. You have a time limit of 60 seconds in which to play the game, so don't waste any time. Use the cursor keys to control your car.

```
  10 REM Death Race
  20 GO SUB 9000: LET hi=0
  30 GO SUB 8000
  40 GO SUB 7000
  50 PRINT AT v,h;" "
  51 IF INKEY$<"5" OR INKEY$>"8"
THEN GO TO 55
  53 LET a$=INKEY$
  55 LET v1=v: LET h1=h
  60 LET v=v+(a$="6")-(a$="7")
  70 LET h=h+(a$="8")-(a$="5")
  80 IF SCREEN$ (v,h)="" THEN GO
TO 1000
  90 IF SCREEN$ (v,h)="_" THEN L
ET v=v1: LET h=h1: LET a$="": GO
TO 55
 100 PRINT AT v,h; INK 3;c$
 105 LET d$=c$
 110 LET c$=("▓" AND a$="7")+("▓
" AND a$="8")+("▓" AND a$="6")+(
"▓" AND a$="5")
 120 IF c$="" THEN LET c$=d$
 125 PRINT AT 21,16;"TIME ";INT
ti;" ": LET ti=ti-.2: IF ti<0 TH
EN GO TO 2000
 130 BEEP .008,sc
 140 PRINT AT j,k;" "
 150 LET j1=j: LET k1=k
 160 LET j=j+INT (RND*3)-1: LET
k=k+INT (RND*3)-1
 170 IF SCREEN$ (j,k)="_" THEN L
ET j=j1: LET k=k1: GO TO 150
 175 IF SCREEN$ (j,k)="" THEN GO
TO 1000
 180 PRINT AT j,k; INK 5;"▓"
 200 GO TO 50
```

67

```
1000 PRINT AT j,k;"▓"
1010 FOR a=1 TO 3
1020 LET sc=sc+1
1030 PRINT AT 21,0;"SCORE ";sc
1040 BEEP .7,sc
1050 NEXT a
1060 LET j=4: LET k=20: LET v=10
: LET k=16: GO TO 40
2000 PRINT AT 21,16; PAPER 2;"TI
ME 0": BEEP 2,-10: CLS
2010 PRINT AT 2,12; PAPER 1;"GAM
E OVER"
2020 PRINT AT 5,10; PAPER 2;"YOU
 SCORED ";sc
2030 IF sc>hi THEN LET hi=sc
2040 PRINT AT 18,6; PAPER 6;"HIG
HEST SCORE TODAY ";hi
2050 INPUT PAPER 1;"PRESS "; PAP
ER 2;"ENTER"; PAPER 1;" TO PLAY
AGAIN "; LINE a$: GO TO 30
7000 CLS : PRINT INVERSE 1; INK
6;"‗
‗‗‗‗‗‗‗‗‗‗‗‗‗‗‗‗‗‗‗‗‗‗‗‗‗‗‗‗‗‗‗‗‗
7010 FOR a=1 TO 19
7020 PRINT INVERSE 1; INK 6;"_";
AT a,31;"_"
```

```
7030 NEXT a
7040 PRINT INVERSE 1; INK 6;"___
___
7050 PRINT AT 21,0;"SCORE ";sc
7060 RETURN
8000 BORDER 0: PAPER 0: INK 9: C
LS
8010 LET v=10: LET h=16
8020 LET j=4: LET k=20
8030 LET sc=0: LET ti=60
8040 LET c$="■"
8050 LET a$=""
8990 RETURN
9000 FOR a=USR "a" TO USR "f"+7
9010 READ user: POKE a,user
9020 NEXT a: RETURN
9030 DATA 60,153,255,153,24,189,
255,189
9040 DATA 238,68,229,255,255,229
,68,238
9050 DATA 189,255,189,24,153,255
,153,60
9060 DATA 119,34,167,255,255,167
,34,119
9070 DATA 56,124,238,198,238,238
,254,254
9080 DATA 56,56,16,124,16,16,40,
68
9998 REM a b c d e f
9999 REM ■ ■ ■ ■ ■ ■
```

DRAUGHTS

This game of draughts, or checkers, is played by conventional rules. Each player starts with 12 pieces and you play on an eight by eight chequered board. Play is confined to the black squares and all the moves are diagonal. You can only move your pieces up the board and the computer can only move down — that is, until you reach the far side of the board and become a 'King' which can move in either direction. You 'take' any pieces that you jump over.

YOU PLAY WHITE AGAINST THE COMPUTER PLAYING BLACK

To make a move you must enter the letter and number of the square you want to move from (C6 for instance); next press ENTER and then enter the number and letter of the square you want to move to (E4 for instance). If you capture one of the computer's pieces it will disappear automatically from the board and you will be asked (a question mark will appear) if you can jump again. Enter 'Y' and press ENTER to make your next jump.

TO PLAY THIS GAME ALL LETTERS MUST BE ENTERED IN UPPER CASE; IT IS EASIER TO PUT THE COMPUTER INTO CAPS-LOCK BEFORE RUNNING THE PROGRAM.

```
   10 REM Draughts/Checkers
   20 GO SUB 9000
   30 GO SUB 1620
   40 GO TO 1340
   50 CLS
   60 PRINT PAPER 1;TAB 12;"CHECK
ERS";
   70 PRINT
   80 PRINT TAB 2; PAPER 6;"ABCDE
FGH"
   90 GO SUB 460
  100 PRINT "Your score ";sm,"Mac
hines score ";si;" "
  110 PRINT
  120 IF u$="N" THEN GO TO 680
  130 IF si=12 THEN PRINT "I win
": STOP
  140 IF sm=12 THEN PRINT "You wi
n ": STOP
  150 REM
  160 IF q=2 THEN GO TO 410
  170 PRINT "Last to ";f$;
  180 INPUT " from (Let.,No.)";c$
;" to ";b$
  220 LET f$=b$
  230 LET d$=c$
  240 GO SUB 1550
  250 LET c=m(i)
  260 IF i=0 THEN GO TO 180
  270 LET d$=b$
  280 GO SUB 1550
  290 LET b=m(i)
  300 IF i=0 THEN GO TO 180
  310 IF ABS (c-b)=10 OR ABS (c-b
)=8 THEN LET sm=sm+1
  320 LET u$=" "
  330 IF b-c=10 THEN LET a(b-5)=0
  340 IF b-c=8 THEN LET a(b-4)=0
  350 IF c-b=10 THEN LET a(c-5)=0
  360 IF c-b=8 THEN LET a(c-4)=0
  370 LET a(b)=a(c)
  380 LET a(c)=0
  390 LET q=2
  400 GO TO 50
  410 LET u$="": LET q=0
  420 IF ABS (c-b)=10 OR ABS (c-b
)=8 THEN PRINT : PRINT : PRINT :
PRINT : INPUT u$
  440 IF u$<>"Y" THEN GO TO 680
  450 GO TO 50
  470 LET m1=0: LET k=1
  480 LET j=-1
  490 FOR i=40 TO 6 STEP -1
  500 IF a(i)=1 AND i>37 THEN LET
a(i)=2
  510 IF a(i)=-1 AND i<10 THEN LE
```

```
T a(i)=-2
  520 IF i=14 OR i=32 OR i=23 THE
N GO TO 580
  530 IF m1=0 THEN PRINT k;" ";:
LET m1=0: LET k=k+1: LET j=-1+j:
 IF j=1 THEN PRINT INK 2;"■";
  540 LET a=a(i)
  550 GO SUB 610
  560 IF m1<>3 OR j=-1 THEN PRINT
 INK 2;"■";
  570 LET m1=m1+1: IF m1>3 THEN L
ET m1=0: PRINT
  580 NEXT i
  590 PRINT
  600 RETURN
  610 REM Print pieces
  620 IF a=0 THEN PRINT " ";
  630 IF a=1 THEN PRINT "■";
  640 IF a=-1 THEN PRINT "O";
  650 IF a=-2 THEN PRINT INVERSE
1;"O";
  660 IF a=2 THEN PRINT INVERSE 1
;"■";
  670 RETURN
  680 LET u$="   ": LET q=0
  690 LET z=6
  700 IF z<9 THEN GO TO 740
  710 IF a(z)<0 AND (a(z-4)=1 OR
a(z-4)=2) AND a(z-8)=0 THEN GO T
O 930
  720 IF z<11 THEN GO TO 740
  730 IF a(z)<0 AND (a(z-5)=1 OR
a(z-5)=2) AND a(z-10)=0 THEN GO
TO 1030
  740 IF z>25 THEN GO TO 770
  750 IF a(z)=-2 AND (a(z+4)=1 OR
a(z+4)=2) AND a(z+8)=0 THEN GO
TO 1140
  760 IF a(z)=-2 AND (a(z+5)=1 OR
a(z+5)=2) AND a(z+10)=0 THEN GO
TO 1250
  770 LET z=z+1: IF z<=40 THEN GO
 TO 700
  780 REM * RANDOM *
  790 LET u=0
  800 LET z=6+INT (RND*34)+1
  810 LET k=0
  820 LET u=u+1
  830 IF a(z)<0 AND a(z-4)=0 THEN
 LET k=1
  840 IF a(z)<0 AND a(z-5)=0 AND
k=0 THEN LET k=2
  850 IF k=0 AND z<26 AND a(z)=-2
 AND a(z+4)=0 THEN LET k=-7
  860 IF z<10 THEN GO TO 880
```

```
 870 IF (k=1 OR k=2) AND v<200 A
ND (a(z-(10 AND z)10))=1 OR a(z-
8)=1) THEN GO TO 800
 880 IF k=0 AND v<400 THEN GO TO
 800
 890 IF k=0 THEN LET sm=12: GO T
O 50
 900 LET a(z-(3+k))=a(z)
 910 LET a(z)=0
 920 GO TO 50
 930 LET a(z-8)=a(z)
 940 LET a(z)=0
 950 LET a(z-4)=0
 960 LET si=si+1
 970 IF z<24 THEN GO TO 50
 980 IF (a(z-13)=1 OR a(z-13)=2)
 AND a(z-18)=0 THEN LET p=2
 990 IF p=1 THEN LET a(z-18)=a(z
-8): LET a(z-13)=00
1000 IF p=2 THEN LET a(z-12)=0:
LET a(z-12)=0
1010 IF p>0 THEN LET a(z-8)=0
1020 GO TO 50
1030 LET a(z-10)=a(z)
1040 LET a(z)=0
1050 LET a(z-5)=0
1060 LET si=si+1
1070 IF z<25 THEN GO TO 50
1080 IF (a(z-15)=1 OR a(z-15)=2)
 AND a(z-20)=0 THEN LET p=1
1090 IF (a(z-14)=1 OR a(z-14)=2)
 AND a(z-18)=0 THEN LET p=2
1100 IF p=1 THEN LET a(z-15)=0:
LET a(z-20)=a(z-10)
1110 IF p=2 THEN LET a(z-14)=0:
LET a(z-18)=a(z-10)
1120 IF p>0 THEN LET a(z-10)=0
1130 GO TO 50
1140 LET a(z+8)=-2
1150 LET a(z+4)=0
1160 LET a(z)=0
1170 LET si=si+1
1180 IF z<32 AND (a(z+3)=1 OR a(
z+3)=2) AND a(z-2)=0 THEN LET p=
1
1190 IF z<23 AND (a(z+14)=1 OR a
(z+14)=2) AND a(z+16)=2 THEN LET
 p=2
1200 IF z<23 AND (a(z+13)=1 OR a
(z+13)=2) AND a(z+18)=0 THEN LET
 p=3
1210 IF p=1 THEN LET a(z+3)=0: L
ET a(z-2)=-2
1220 IF p=2 THEN LET a(z+14)=0:
LET a(z+16)=0
```

```
1230 IF p=3 THEN LET a(z+13)=0:
LET a(z+18)=-2
1240 IF p>0 THEN LET a(z+8)=0
1250 LET a(z+10)=-2
1260 LET a(z+5)=0
1270 LET a(z)=0
1280 LET si=si+1
1290 GO TO 50
1300 PRINT : PRINT
1310 PRINT : PRINT
1320 RETURN
1330 REM * INITIALISE *
1340 DIM a(45)
1350 PRINT
1360 FOR z=1 TO 45
1370 IF z<6 THEN LET a(z)=9
1380 IF z>5 AND z<19 THEN LET a(
z)=1
1390 IF z>18 AND z<28 THEN LET a
(z)=0
1400 IF z>27 AND z<41 THEN LET a
(z)=-1
1410 IF z>40 THEN LET a(z)=9
1420 NEXT z
1430 LET a(14)=9: LET a(23)=9: L
ET a(32)=9
1440 LET f$="--"
1450 LET p=0: LET q=0
1460 LET si=0: LET sm=0
1470 PRINT : PRINT
1480 INPUT "Do you want the firs
t move y/n"; LINE q$
1490 LET u$=""
1500 PRINT
1510 IF q$<>"Y" THEN GO TO 550
1520 LET u$=""
1530 PRINT
1540 GO TO 50
1550 REM Decode move
1560 LET i=1
1570 IF m$(i)=d$ THEN GO TO 1610
1580 LET i=i+1
1590 IF i=33 THEN LET i=0: GO TO
 1610
1600 GO TO 1570
1610 RETURN
1620 DIM m$(32,2): DIM m(32)
1630 DATA "B1","D1","F1","H1","B
2","C2","E2","G2","B3","D3","F3"
,"H3","A4","C4","E4","G4","B5","
D5","F5","H5","A6","C6","E6","E6"
1640 DATA "G6","B7","D7","F7","H
7","A8","C8","E8","G8"
1650 DATA 40,39,38,37,36,35,34,3
3,31,30
```

```
1660 DATA 29,28,27,26,25,24,22,2
1,20,19
1670 DATA 18,17,16,15,13,12,11,1
0,9,8,7,6
1675 RESTORE 1630
1680 FOR i=1 TO 32
1690 READ m$(i)
1700 NEXT i
1710 FOR i=1 TO 32
1720 READ m(i)
1730 NEXT i
1740 RETURN
9000 BORDER 0: PAPER 0: INK 9: C
LS
9005 RESTORE 9030: FOR a=USR "a"
 TO USR "a"+7
9010 READ user: POKE a,user
9020 NEXT a: RETURN
9030 DATA 0,60,126,126,126,126,6
0,0
9998 REM a
9999 REM ▓
```

75

SIMON SAID

This is a version of the toy of the same name. The computer selects a sequence of colours, with accompanying sounds, and you must repeat the sequence exactly. There are four different colours. The sequence begins with one randomly selected colour and each time the sequence is repeated another colour is added. The maximum length of the sequence is from one to ten.

```
 10 REM Simon Said...
 20 REM Tim Hartnell
      Peter Shaw
 30 GO SUB 9000: GO SUB 8000
 40 FOR a=1 TO 10
 50 LET c$=c$+STR$ (INT (RND*4)
+1)
 60 NEXT a
 70 FOR q=1 TO x
 80 LET l=4*(CODE c$(q)-48)
 90 LET t=VAL c$(q)
100 BEEP .05,10*t
110 PRINT AT l,7; INK 6;" ██ ";I
NT l/4;AT l-1,7;" ▄▄ ";AT l+1,7;"
▀▀ "
120 PAUSE 4
130 CLS
140 NEXT q
150 FOR b=1 TO x
160 IF INKEY$<>"" THEN GO TO 16
0
170 LET t$=INKEY$
180 IF CODE t$=0 THEN GO TO 170
190 CLS
200 LET y=4*(CODE t$-48)
210 PRINT AT y,7; INK y/4;" ██ "
; INK 6;t$;AT y-1,7; INK y/4;" ▄▄
▄ ";AT y+1,7;" ▀▀ "
220 BEEP .04,2.5*y
230 IF CODE t$<>CODE (c$(b)) TH
EN GO TO 1000
240 PAUSE 7
250 CLS
260 NEXT b
270 IF x=10 THEN PRINT "You def
eat the machine!": INPUT "Press
```

```
Enter to play again "; LINE a$:
RUN
  280 LET x=x+1
  290 PAUSE 50
  300 GO TO 70
1000 PRINT "You scored ";x-1
1010 BEEP .02,RND*30
1020 INPUT "Press Enter to play
again ", LINE a$: RUN
8000 BORDER 0: PAPER 0: INK 7: C
LS : BRIGHT 1
8010 LET c$=""
8020 LET x=1
8990 RETURN
9000 FOR a=USR "a" TO USR "d"+7
9010 READ user: POKE a,user
9020 NEXT a: RETURN
9030 DATA 0,0,0,0,3,7,15,15
9040 DATA 0,0,0,0,192,224,240,24
0
9050 DATA 15,15,7,3,0,0,0,0
9060 DATA 240,240,224,192,0,0,0,
0
```

77

3D DRIVER

This is a spectral adaptation of the arcade driver games. You are given a 3D view of your car and the road in perspective. The road moves from side to side, and you must avoid crashing into the side of the road. Use the cursor keys 5 and 8 to control your car.

```
  10 REM 3D Driver
  20 GO SUB 9000
  30 GO SUB 8000
  40 PRINT AT 15,15; INK 4;" ";
AT 16,15;" "
  50 IF p<108 OR p>150 THEN GO T
O 1000
  60 PLOT p-10,159: DRAW -170+(p
-10),-159
  70 PLOT p+10,159: DRAW -70+(p-
10),-159
  80 PLOT OVER 1;p-10,159: DRAW
OVER 1;-170+(p-10),-159
  90 PLOT OVER 1;p+10,159: DRAW
OVER 1;-70+(p-10),-159
  100 LET p=p+4*(INKEY$="5")-4*(I
NKEY$="8")
  110 LET p=p+(INT (RND*20)-10)
  115 LET sc=sc+1
  120 GO TO 50
  990 STOP
1000 PLOT p-10,159: DRAW -170+(p
-10),-159
1010 PLOT p+10,159: DRAW -70+(p-
10),-159
1020 PRINT AT 15,15; FLASH 1; IN
K 2;" ";AT 16,15;" "
1030 FOR a=0 TO 50: BEEP .05,-a:
 BEEP .008,a: NEXT a
1040 PRINT AT 1,10; PAPER 1;"You
 scored ";sc
1050 INPUT "Press "; INK 6;"ENTE
R"; INK 7;" to play again "; LIN
E a$: GO TO 30
8000 BORDER 0: PAPER 0: INK 7: C
LS
8010 LET p=127
8020 LET sc=0
```

```
8040 PRINT AT 0,0; PAPER 1;"

8990 RETURN
9000 FOR a=USR "a" TO USR "d"+7
9010 READ user: POKE a,user
9020 NEXT a: RETURN
9030 DATA 0,0,0,0,13,11,13,3
9040 DATA 0,0,0,0,176,208,176,19
2
9050 DATA 6,117,207,223,208,240,
12,3
9060 DATA 102,174,243,251,19,15,
48,192
9998 REM ab
       cd
9999 REM
```

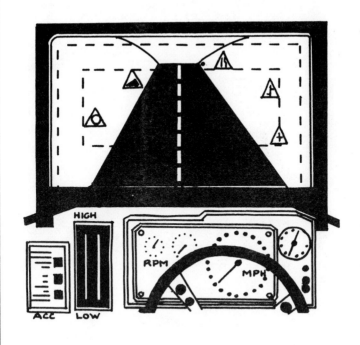

DROP OUT

This is a relatively simple game. A ball is placed at the top of a high plateau; you have to estimate the force required to make it fall into the hole at the bottom of the screen. You do this by entering a number between one and nine into the computer.

This program should help you to estimate the distances on the screen, which will be of use when you come to write programs where the text has to be lined up in the centre.

```
 10 REM Drop out
 20 GO SUB 9000
 30 GO SUB 8000
 40 GO SUB 7000
 50 INPUT "Force ? "; LINE a$:
IF a$>"9" OR a$<"1" THEN GO TO 5
0
 60 FOR a=0 TO 8
 70 PRINT AT 3,a;"●"
 80 BEEP .1,a
110 PRINT AT 3,a;" ": NEXT a
120 FOR a=4 TO 15
130 PRINT AT a,8;"●"
140 BEEP .1,a
170 LET b=b+.5
180 PRINT AT a,8;" "
190 LET a=a+b
200 NEXT a
210 PRINT AT 15,8;"●"
220 BEEP .2,5
230 PRINT AT 15,8; INK 1;"L"
240 FOR a=1 TO VAL a$*2
250 PRINT AT 15,8+a;"●"
260 BEEP .1,a
290 PRINT AT 15,8+a;" "
300 NEXT a
310 IF VAL a$=b THEN PRINT AT 1
5,8+(b*2);"●": LET sc=sc+1: PRIN
T AT 21,20; PAPER 6; INK 9;"SCOR
E ";sc: BEEP 1,30
315 BEEP 1,10
320 GO TO 40
7000 REM
```

```
7010 FOR a=4 TO 15
7020 PRINT AT a,0; INK 1;"
"
7030 NEXT a
7040 FOR a=16 TO 21
7050 PRINT INK 1;"
"
7060 NEXT a
7070 PRINT AT 15,8; INK 1;"L"
7080 LET h=INT (RND*9)+1
7090 PRINT AT 16,8+(h*2);" "
7100 RETURN
8000 LET sc=0
8010 BORDER 0: PAPER 0: INK 6: C
LS
8020 LET b=.5
8990 RETURN
9000 FOR a=USR "a" TO USR "b"+7
9010 READ user: POKE a,user
9020 NEXT a: RETURN
9030 DATA 60,126,255,255,255,255
,126,60
9050 DATA 128,128,128,128,128,12
8,224,255
9980 REM a b
9990 REM ● L
```

DROP OUT
O
O
O
O

M4

Rushing across the M4 motorway in rush hour is not everybody's idea of fun, but that is the point of this game. Two lanes of cars, going in opposite directions, have to be avoided; if you are hit by a vehicle then you lose one of your five lives. You score 10 points for every man safely home. There is a high score feature. Use the cursor keys to control your movement.

```
  10 REM M4
  20 GO SUB 9000: LET hi=0
  30 GO SUB 8000
  40 LET v=14: LET h=16: GO SUB
7000
  50 PRINT AT v,h; PAPER 8;" "
  60 LET v=v+(INKEY$="6" AND v<2
1)-(INKEY$="7" AND v>0)
  70 LET h=h+(INKEY$="8" AND h<3
1)-(INKEY$="5" AND h>0)
  80 PRINT AT 4,0; INK 6;a$;AT 2
1,0;b$;AT 5,0;b$;AT 12,0;a$
  90 IF SCREEN$ (v,h)="" THEN GO
TO 1000
 100 PRINT AT v,h; PAPER 8;"Ï"
 110 LET b$=b$(32)+b$( TO 31)
 120 LET a$=a$(2 TO )+a$(1)
 130 IF v=2 THEN GO TO 2000
 150 GO TO 50
1000 PRINT AT v,h; FLASH 1;"Ï"
1010 DIM s$(1,704)
1020 PRINT AT 0,0; FLASH 8; OVER
1; PAPER 8; INK 2;s$(1)
1025 IF m>0 THEN LET m=m-1: G
O TO 40
1026 IF sc>hi THEN LET hi=sc
1030 INPUT "Press ENTER to play
again "; LINE b$
1040 GO TO 30
2000 LET sc=sc+10
2010 GO TO 40
7000 CLS
7010 PRINT 'TAB 12;"HIGH ";hi;TA
B 23;"SCORE ";sc;' PAPER 1;"
          "
7020 PRINT INK 6'a$'b$
7030 PRINT ' PAPER 4;"
```

82

```
7050 PRINT INK 6´b$´a$
7060 PRINT ´ PAPER 1;"

7070 PRINT AT v,h; PAPER 3;"⅟"
7080 FOR a=1 TO ml: PRINT AT 1,a
; INK 5;"⅟";: NEXT a
7090 RETURN
8000 BORDER 0: PAPER 0: INK 9: C
LS
8010 LET sc=0
8030 LET a$="
8040 LET b$="
8060 LET ml=5
8990 RETURN
9000 FOR a=USR "a" TO USR "a"+7
9010 READ user: POKE a,user
9020 NEXT a: RETURN
9030 DATA 0,1,2,127,235,253,28,5
9040 DATA 0,240,16,252,215,187,5
6,16
9050 DATA 0,15,8,63,235,221,28,8
9060 DATA 0,128,64,254,215,191,2
8,8
9070 DATA 28,28,8,8,62,8,28,34
```

83

HANGMAN

This is a version of the well known word game. The computer displays a number of dashes corresponding to the number of letters in the word. You then enter a letter, and if that letter is in the word the letter is displayed and you have your next guess. If your guess is wrong the computer starts to print the poor man about to be hanged. You have 13 chances before the man is put to death, so don't just run through the alphabet in sequence as it is unlikely you will get the word.

When you choose your letter and enter it in the computer, the computer will put in all instances of that letter: carrot, for instance, has two r's, so both would be entered by the computer. As you can see by the listing, this program has an extensive dictionary, so the person who is typing in the program can still play the game without knowing at once the word chosen.

```
  10 REM Hangman
  20 GO SUB 9000
  30 GO SUB 8000
  40 GO SUB 7000
  50 FOR a=1 TO LEN w$
  60 PRINT "_ ";
  70 NEXT a
  80 INPUT "Guess (only 1 letter
) "; LINE n$
  90 LET r=0: FOR a=1 TO LEN w$
 100 IF w$(a)=n$ THEN LET r=r+1
 110 NEXT a
 120 IF r<>0 THEN GO TO 1000
 130 LET t$=t$+n$+" "
 140 GO SUB 6000
 150 LET c$="": FOR a=1 TO LEN w
$: LET d$=SCREEN$ (0,(a*2)-2): L
ET c$=c$+d$: NEXT a: IF c$=w$ TH
EN GO TO 5000
 160 GO TO 30
1000 FOR a=1 TO LEN w$
1010 IF w$(a)=n$ THEN PRINT AT 0
,(a*2)-2;n$
1020 NEXT a
1030 GO TO 150
2000 PRINT AT 5,19;"|": BEEP 1,-
10
2010 PRINT AT 5,0;"You killed hi
m!"
2011 PRINT AT 7,0;"the word was.
";AT 8,0;w$
2020 INPUT "Press enter to play
again "; LINE j$: GO TO 30
5000 PRINT AT 5,0;"Got it!"
5010 INPUT "Press enter to play
again "; LINE j$: GO TO 30
6000 LET d=d+2: LET h=h+2: IF h>
31 THEN LET v=v+1: LET h=18
6010 PRINT AT v,h; INK 4;n$
6020 PRINT AT INT (d/2)+2-5,17;
INK 6;b$(INT ((d-16)/2))
6030 IF INT ((d-16)/2)=13 THEN G
O TO 2000
6040 RETURN
7000 RESTORE 7000
7005 FOR a=1 TO INT (RND*193)+1
7010 READ w$
7020 NEXT a
7030 DATA "airship","aircraft","
ape","anvil","apply","artic","ar
my","arthropod","barrow","binary
","birch","bizzare","bite","blis
ter","blood","bobtail","bradawl"
,"brain","camera","canoe","cap",
"care","castanets","catch","cell
```

```
","chapel","chariot","classic","
coach"
7040 DATA "doublet","duckling","
dune","dual","dwarf","embank","e
mploy","encounter","engine","enl
iven","envelope","equinox","fade
","feel","fence","fill","finish"
,"fish","flag"
7050 DATA "gauge","gear","geomet
ry","glassy","gnu","gold","gradu
s","grudge","heart","head","heli
copter","heraldry","hospital","h
overcraft","ice","imperial","inf
low","jib","jersey","joiner","ju
venile","kale","kennel","knell",
"labarum","landau","lathe","lead
er","leghorn","light","lip"
7060 DATA "mass","match","maze",
"medium","mellow","melt","mill",
"moon","motor","mount","mystify"
,"nerve","niche","nostalgia","ob
ject","once","optical","orange",
"orb","ordinary","orphan","obtus
e","oversea","ozone"
7070 DATA "pall","pancake","pant
ograph","parcel","parallax","par
liment","particle","phaeton","pi
ck","pillory","plaice","plane","
pleat","poetry","postage","pound
","project","propeller","quadril
le","quilt","queue","quote","rab
bit","raffle","reciprocal"
7080 DATA "remand","remain","res
idence","revenue","roach","savag
e","sage","scarp","scare","scurf
y","sea","second","semaphore","s
entence","shampoo"
7090 DATA "tassel","tatty","tazz
a","teeter","teller","tennis","t
ension","tetanus","thick","tick"
,"tiger","titanic","toast","toni
c","torrid","tribe","umpire","un
couth","understate","unruly","un
seat","urge"
7100 DATA "vacuum","valentine","
vagrant","valve","variable","vau
lt","vein","visit","wage","walle
t","warn","warning","water","wax
","weapon","wells","whale","whir
l","whippet","whistle","xylophon
e","year","youth","yolk","zany",
"zebra","zoom","zoologist"
7110 RETURN
8000 BORDER 0: PAPER 0: INK 2: C
LS
```

```
8010  DIM  b$(13,5)
8020  LET  b$(1) =  "          "
8030  LET  b$(2) =  "          "
8040  LET  b$(3) =  "          "
8050  LET  b$(4) =  "          "
8060  LET  b$(5) =  "          "
8070  LET  b$(6) =  "          "
8080  LET  b$(7) =  "          "
8090  LET  b$(8) =  "          "
8100  LET  b$(9) =  "          "
8110  LET  b$(10) ="          "
8120  LET  b$(11) ="          "
8130  LET  b$(12) ="          "
8140  LET  b$(13) ="   n  n   "
8150  LET  t$=""
8160  LET  h=16:  LET  v=0
8170  LET  d=16
8990  RETURN
9000  RESTORE 9000: FOR a=USR "a"
      TO USR "9"+7
9010  READ user: POKE a,user
9020  NEXT a: RETURN
9030  DATA 0,0,0,7,15,28,24,24
9040  DATA 24,24,28,15,7,0,0,0
9050  DATA 0,0,0,224,240,56,24,24
9060  DATA 24,24,56,240,224,0,0,0
9070  DATA 0,0,0,255,255,0,0,0
9080  DATA 24,24,24,24,24,24,24,2
      4
9090  DATA 0,0,102,102,0,0,0,0
```

87

VIDEO SALESMAN

How long can you last in the cut and thrust world of Video salesmanship? In this program you buy and sell Video Recorders to make a profit. You buy Video Recorders at £200 each, then choose the price to sell them at. The number of recorders you sell in any week depends on the selling price and on the situation of the Video market (this is displayed by the computer before each turn).

You should be careful when buying stock since if you fail to sell the recorders one week you cannot sell them the next week. The game lasts for five weeks and you start out with a capital of £1,000.

```
  10 REM Video Salesman
  20 REM
  30 GO SUB 8000
  40 INPUT AT 22,0;AT 0,6;"How m
any players "; LINE p$;AT 18,6;"
Press ENTER to play";AT 22,30; L
INE a$
  50 LET p=VAL p$: IF p<1 THEN G
O TO 40
  55 DIM s(p): DIM c(p): FOR a=1
 TO p: LET c(a)=1000: NEXT a
  60 FOR w=1 TO 5
  70 FOR l=1 TO p
  75 IF c(l)<200 THEN PRINT "Sal
esman ";l,,"You have not got eno
ugh money tobuy any stock": NEXT
 l: NEXT w: GO TO 270
  80 CLS
  90 PRINT "Salesman ";l,"Sales
";s(l)
  95 PRINT '"Cash in hand ";c(l)
 100 GO SUB 2000
 110 PRINT '"Local & National ne
ws :-"
 120 PRINT h$
```

```
 130 INPUT AT 15,0;AT 0,0;"How m
any recorders will you    stock
 this week (£200 ea) ";re;AT 5,0
;"How much will you charge per
 recorder ";ch;AT 15,5;"Press E
NTER to continue"; LINE a$
 135 IF re*200>c(l) THEN GO TO 1
30
 140 CLS
 150 PRINT "Salesman ";l
 160 LET sa=(h*(10)/(ch/10))
 170 IF sa>re THEN LET sa=re
 180 PRINT ''"Cash in hand ";c(l)
 190 LET s(l)=INT sa
 200 PRINT ''"Sales this week ";s
(l)
 210 LET pr=(s(l)*ch)-(re*200)
 220 PRINT ''"Profit ";pr
 230 LET c(l)=c(l)+pr
 240 PRINT "New balance ";c(l)
 250 INPUT "Press enter to conti
nue "; LINE a$: NEXT l
 260 NEXT w
 990 STOP
2000 LET h=INT (RND*20)+1
2010 IF h>10 THEN GO TO 2500
2020 RESTORE 2000
2030 FOR a=1 TO INT (RND*6)+1: R
EAD h$: NEXT a
2040 RETURN
2050 DATA "This is World Cup wee
k!","E.T. has just been release
d on video officialy","Video rec
orders go down in price","Specia
l offer on Blank tapes","It's ge
tting near Christmas","New video
 tape hire shop opens  in town"
2500 RESTORE 2500
2510 FOR a=1 TO INT (RND*5)+1: R
EAD h$: NEXT a
2520 RETURN
2530 DATA "Inflation hits video
industry","Cheap video discs bec
ome popular","Cable television c
uts sales","Cinema has increased
 popularity","Slump in video ind
ustry"
8000 BORDER 0: PAPER 0: INK 9: C
LS
9990 RETURN
```

DAM BUSTERS

While flying back from a mission in Europe you have
engine trouble and begin to lose altitude. The only safe
place to land is in the river. Unfortunately there is a Dam
in your way, so you will have to blow this up. Use the Ø key
to drop your bombs.

```
10 REM Dam Busters
20 GO SUB 9000: LET hi=0
30 GO SUB 8000
40 GO SUB 7000
50 FOR v=1 TO 15
55 PRINT AT v-1,0; PAPER 8;"
   "
60 FOR h=0 TO 31
70 PRINT AT v,h; INK 6; PAPER
8;"     "
80 IF SCREEN$ (v,h+5)<>" " THE
N GO TO 1000
90 IF INKEY$="0" THEN GO SUB 2
00
95 LET sc=sc+1
100 BEEP (.008 AND ch=1)+(.01 A
ND ch=0),0
105 IF ch=0 THEN GO TO 120
110 IF (SCREEN$ (13,16)=" " AND
 SCREEN$ (13,17)=" " AND SCREEN$
 (13,18)=" ") THEN LET ch=0: PRI
NT AT 13,0;"        ";AT
 14,20; INK 2; PAPER 1;"▚
   ";AT 13,16; PAPER 0;"   "
180 NEXT h
190 NEXT v
195 GO TO 1500
200 PRINT AT v+1,h; INK 5; PAPE
R 8;" ▶"
210 PRINT AT v,h; PAPER 8; INK
6;"     "
220 LET h=h+1: IF h>30 THEN LET
 v=v+1: LET h=0
240 PRINT AT v+1,h; INK 5; PAPE
R 8;" ◀"
```

90

```
 250 PRINT AT v,h; PAPER 8; INK
6;" "
 260 LET h=h+1: IF h>31 THEN LET
v=v+1: LET h=0
 275 PRINT AT v+2,h; PAPER 8;" "
 280 LET b1=h
 290 FOR b=v+1 TO 14
 295 BEEP .01,b
 300 PRINT AT b,b1; PAPER 8; INK
5;" ";AT b+1,b1;"$"
 310 PRINT AT v,h; INK 6; PAPER
8;" "
 320 LET h=h+1: IF h>30 THEN LET
v=v+1: LET h=0
 330 IF SCREEN$ (b+2,b1)<>" " TH
EN GO TO 500
 335 PRINT AT v-1,31;" "
 340 NEXT b
 350 PRINT AT b,b1; PAPER 8;" "
 360 LET h=h-1
 380 RETURN
 500 FOR b=b TO b+1
 510 PRINT AT b,b1; PAPER 8;" ";
AT b+1,b1; INK 5;"$"
 520 NEXT b
 524 BEEP .005,-b
 525 LET h=h-1: PRINT AT b,b1; P
APER 8;" "
 530 RETURN
1000 FOR a=v TO 15
1010 PRINT AT a,h+1; PAPER 1;"
 ";AT a+1,h+1; INK 6;" "
1020 BEEP .5,-a: NEXT a
1030 GO TO 1510
1500 LET sc=sc+100: PRINT AT 0,1
2;"GAME OVER"
1510 PRINT AT 5,12;"You scored "
;sc
1520 IF sc>hi THEN LET hi=sc
1530 PRINT AT 10,6;"Highest scor
e today ";hi
1540 INPUT "Press ENTER to play
again "; LINE a$: GO TO 30
7000 CLS
7010 PRINT AT 13,0; PAPER 1;"
 "
7020 PRINT AT 14,0; PAPER 1;"
 "
7030 PRINT AT 15,0; PAPER 1;"
 "
7040 PRINT AT 12,16; INK 2;" ",
AT 13,16; PAPER 1;" "; PAPER 0;
" ";AT 14,16; PAPER 1;" "; PA
PER 0;" ";AT 15,16; PAPER 1;"
 "
```

91

```
7050 FOR a=1 TO 4
7060 PRINT PAPER 2;"
7070 NEXT a
7990 RETURN
8000 BORDER 0: PAPER 0: INK 9: C
LS
8010 LET sc=0
8020 LET ch=1
8990 RETURN
9000 FOR a=USR "a" TO USR "i"+7
9010 READ user: POKE a,user
9020 NEXT a: RETURN
9030 DATA 56,60,63,63,63,7,0,0
9040 DATA 0,0,128,255,255,255,25
5,0
9050 DATA 0,0,63,255,255,255,255
,0
9060 DATA 0,0,224,248,248,248,24
0,0
9070 DATA 0,0,220,126,126,220,0,
0
9080 DATA 0,0,28,254,30,14,0,0
9090 DATA 36,60,24,60,60,24,0,0
9100 DATA 128,192,224,240,248,25
2,254,255
9110 DATA 254,255,255,255,255,25
5,255,255
9990 REM a b c d e f g h i
9999 REM
```

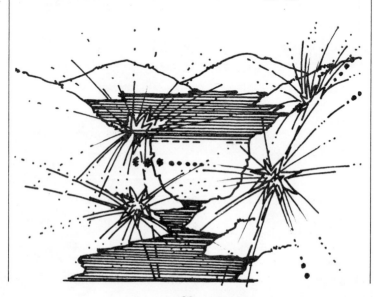

How To Write Better Programs

By Tim Hartnell, series editor

There are a number of fine programs in this book, and many of the regular computer magazines contain other such ones. But no matter how good the programs from published sources are, you are certain to get more pleasure from running them if they have been partially or completely written by you. Putting your personal stamp on programs, altering them to reflect your wishes and creativity, is an excellent way to improve the programs, and eventually, of course, you'll become a better and more imaginative programmer.

Programs in magazines, and in books like this one, are ideal as starting points for your own developments. You may also find that advertisements for software packages can be fruitful 'idea-starters'. You only need to read the description of what the commercially available program does, and you will have the first step towards creating your own program. You have to be careful, of course, not to infringe copyright either in the screen displays, in the name of the program, or the names of the 'characters' within the program. However, you will probably find that at a certain point in its development the program will take on a life of its own, growing and evolving away from the original scenario, until you eventually have a completely new game concept and implementation.

Whatever you do, be careful not to pass off other people's work as your own. By all means adapt and improve published programs, but do not then present them to magazines as if they were originals. I have lost count of the number of times one of my own programs, from one of my books, has been submitted to me for publication.

Always watch out for new ideas as you look through books, game and computer magazines, or wander through video game arcades. It may be worth keeping notes of ideas you come across for games, for character shapes, for sounds, for dramatic endings and so on. Thus you will never be short of ideas, and you will also be able to merge the material together to produce better games which hold the player's attention for longer.

Games tend to fall into one of three categories, and it is worth making sure of the category into which your proposed program will fall *before* you start to program, since the category of game materially alters the programming approach. This is not to say that, as you develop a program, it will not move from one category into another, nor that a particular game might not extend across two categories, but it is nevertheless useful to keep the various groups separate in your mind, just to clarify your thoughts. The three categories are:

1. Board games
2. 'Arcade' (that is, highly visual, fast moving, noisy, real time) games
3. Games of chance (such as Roulette and Snap).

In board games, the quality of play is more important than lightning-fast response, while the arcade-type programs must be kept moving at all costs, even if some 'intelligence' from your Martian intruders must be sacrificed to achieve this. Games of chance depend more on their ease of play ('user-friendly' inputs), and an approach to true randomness, than do either of the other categories.

You will find that games programs tend to fall into types, which are subdivisions of the three above mentioned categories. Many board games are variants of chess or checkers; many arcade games started off life as Space Invader-type games; and games of chance

94

started off in the 'real world' of dice and cards. Looking at a program description, or a games machine, and trying to categorise the game you see can help trigger new ideas which fit within that particular game's genre.

There is a school of thought within programming — generally called 'structured programming' — which believes that discipline at the beginning of the games-writing process is essential. While less interesting than sitting down at the computer right away, a much better program is produced in the end. I once wrote a program called Dome Dweller, a simulation program in which the player is in charge of a 'lunar dome' and must decide which products to manufacture and sell in order to buy oxygen and food for the station's inhabitants. (This program was used in my book *The Book of Listings*, written with Jeremy Ruston, and published by the BBC.)Once I had decided the overall scenario, I worked out the screen display, and came up with an idea as follows:

>Oxygen supplies are low
>There are 96 people living within your dome in year 3
>Money credit is $5,693
>Annual maintenance charge is $226
>Oxygen tanks hold 811 units
>Oxygen costs $8 per unit
>Each dome dweller needs 5 units a year
>Food stocks stand at 2122
>Each dweller needs 3 units a year ($6 each, $576 for dome. This will last 7 years at present population.)
>You can trade your unique lunar sculptures with the people who live in other domes. You use up 2 units of oxygen making each one, and sell them for $30.

As you can probably guess from this 'sample printout', the idea of the program is to decide how many 'unique lunar sculptures' you must make and sell in order to buy oxygen and food, and to pay the 'annual maintenance' charge. The problem with this particular program is that making each sculpture uses up oxygen, so you must balance your wish to make money against the need to use the oxygen intelligently.

You may well wish to try writing such a program yourself. You should end up with an enjoyable program, and writing it will do much to help you develop your programming skills. The first thing to do is to make a list of what the program has to do:

> Set up the needed variables
> Tell the player the 'state of the dome'
> Ask how much oxygen to be bought
> Check if can afford this, if so buy it, if not go back and ask again
> Ask how much food to be bought
> Check if can afford this, if so buy it, if not go back and ask again
> Update oxygen quantity
> Update food quantity
> Reduce money left total
> Ask how many items of sculpture to be made
> Check if there is enough oxygen to make this many, if not go back and ask again
> Reduce oxygen quantity by amount needed to make the number of sculptures specified, increase money total to reflect value of sculptures made
> Increase the population total slightly, add one to the 'current year'
> Check if there is enough food in stocks to feed whole population
> Check if there is enough oxygen for whole population
> Check if there is any money
> If any of these conditions are negative (eg not enough food) send action to an 'end of game' routine
> If all are positive, loop back to tell the player the state of the dome, and continue to circle

You could probably write a Dome Dweller program

using the list above, together with the 'sample printout' information. There is, however, a secret I should like to share with you which unlocks programming problems almost instantly. You can actually write all the vital parts of a program in minutes, so you can see the raw framework of a program like this running long before you fill in the details. And once you have a framework you can work on it for as long as you like, knowing as you do so that — at every moment in program development — you have a working program. You do not have to wait until the end until you can run it to see how you are going. The 'secret' is to hold the entire program within a series of subroutine calls, all held within a perpetual loop. Here's how it could work with this program. The very first lines you enter in your computer are as follows:

```
10 REM DOME DWELLER
20 GOSUB 1000: REM ASSIGN VARIABLES
30 GOSUB 2000: REM PRINT OUT STATE OF DOME
40 GOSUB 3000: REM OXYGEN
50 GOSUB 4000: REM FOOD
60 GOSUB 5000: REM SCULPTURE
70 GOSUB 6000: REM UPDATE POPULATION
80 GOSUB 7000: REM CHECK ON STATE OF DOME
90 IF (all conditions positive, from GOSUB 7000) THEN GOTO 30
100 REM End of game ...
```

As you can see once you have the 'master loop' set up in this way, it is relatively simple to fill in each of the subroutines one by one, testing each as you do so, and elaborating each one so that you end up eventually with a very good program. The only thing you need now is a list of the variables which you will use with the program.

I find the best way to do this is to use explicit names for variables so that when you are programming you do not have to spend time checking, for example, whether AA stands for the population, or the number of units of oxygen used up in making each item of sculpture. To make programs as easy as possible to transfer between different computers you can stick to two letter variable names, or you can take advantage (if your computer allows it) of long names (such as OXYUSE for the amount of oxygen used) for variables. Then you have no doubts whatsoever as to the meaning of each variable name. To show how this can work, and to illustrate a further advantage of explicit variable names, here are the variables used in Dome Dweller:

> FOLK — population of dome
> CASH — money in treasury
> FOOD — food stocks on hand
> FOODCOST — how much each unit of food costs
> FOODNEED — how many units of food were consumed per person per year
> ARTCOST — how much oxygen was used up making each piece of sculpture
> ARTPAY — how many dollars each piece of sculpture was sold for
> OXY — oxygen stocks on hand
> OXYNEED — how many units of oxygen were consumed per person per year
> OXYCOST — how much each unit of oxygen cost to buy
> REPAIR — the cost of annual repairs to the dome
> YEAR — the year of the dome's life

Using explicit variable names in this way — although they use up more memory than do single or double-letter variable names — makes it very simple to follow through a program, working out what each section of the program actually does. Moreover, and this is the further advantage mentioned, it is very easy when writing the program to insert the formulae required for calculations. By this I mean that if, for example, you wished to include (as I do in this program) an indication of how much oxygen is needed for each year, you simply multiply the number of people in the dome (FOLK) by the number of oxygen units each person needs each year (OXYNEED). You can then include within the printouts for the state of the dome a line like:

```
PRINT "THERE ARE ";FOLK;" IN THE DOME"
PRINT "IN YEAR ";YEAR
PRINT "EACH PERSON NEEDS ";OXYNEED;"
      UNITS OF"
PRINT "OXYGEN EACH YEAR,";
      OXYNEED*FOLK;" NEEDED"
PRINT "FOR THE WHOLE DOME"
```

It also makes it very easy to check on whether purchases are possible. For example, to buy food, you could say:

```
PRINT "HOW MUCH FOOD WILL YOU BUY?"
INPUT A
IF A*FOODCOST 〉 CASH THEN GOTO (get
another A)
```

So the suggestions given here for improving your programs by the use of 'structured programming' include the following:

- draw up a sample printout, or mock-up of the final screen display

- draw up a list of what the program has to do each time through a 'master control loop'

- change this list to a series of subroutine calls

- use explicit variable names if possible

It is useful if you are designing programs for others to use to ensure that it is quite clear what the player should do when running the program. There is little point, especially when memory is limited, in including a long set of instructions within the program, but you should certainly write such instructions down. In addition, user prompts should be explicit (such as ENTER THE NUMBER OF GOES YOU WANT) and should include warnings of the limits which will be placed on the input (HOW MANY CARDS WILL YOU START WITH: 1, 2 OR 3 ?, for instance).

You cannot assume that you will be present every time a program is run, so you should do your best to make it as foolproof as possible. If you can, add error-trapping routines to the program to ensure that a mistake in entering a choice earlier on in the program will not cause it to crash or come up with stupid results later on.

If you read through this section of the book several times and try to apply the ideas to your own programming work, you should find your work quality improves significantly, and also that you can spend more time improving and embellishing a program and less in the raw mechanical task of getting the thing running.

GLOSSARY

A

Accumulator — the place within the computer in which arithmetic computations are performed and where the results of these computations are stored.

Algorithm — the series of steps the computer follows to solve a particular problem.

Alphanumeric — this term is usually used in relation to a keyboard, as in 'it is an alphanumeric keyboard', which means that the keyboard has letters as well as numbers. It is also used to refer to the 'character set' of the computer. The character set comprises the numbers and letters the computer can print on the screen.

ALU (Arithmetic/Logic Unit) — the part of the computer which does arithmetic (such as addition, subtraction) and where decisions are made.

AND — a Boolean logic operation that the computer uses in its decision-making process. It is based on Boolean algebra, a system developed by mathematician George Boole (1815-64). In Boolean algebra the variables of an expression represent a logical operation such as OR and NOR.

ASCII — stands for American Standard Code for Information Exchange, the most widely used encoding system for English language alphanumerics. There are 128 upper and lower case letters, digits and some special characters. ASCII converts the symbols and control instructions into seven-bit binary combinations.

Assembler — a program which converts other programs written in assembly language into machine code (which the computer can understand directly). Assembly language is a low level programming language which uses easily memorised combinations of two or three letters to represent a particular instruction which the assembler then converts so the machine can understand it. Examples of these are ADD (add), and SUB (subtract). A computer programmed in assembly language tends to work more quickly than one programmed in a higher level language such as BASIC.

B

BASIC — an acronym for Beginners All-Purpose Symbolic Instruction Code. It is the most widely used computer language in the microcomputer field. Although it has been criticised by many people, it has the virtue of being very easy to learn. A great number of BASIC statements resemble ordinary English.

Baud — named after Baudot, a pioneer of telegraphic communications. Baud measures the rate of transfer of information and is approximately equal to one bit per second.

BCD — an abbreviation for Binary Coded Decimal.

Benchmark — a test against which certain functions of the computer can be measured. There are a number of so-called 'standard Benchmark tests', but generally these only test speed. This is rarely the aspect of a microcomputer that is most of interest to the potential buyer.

Binary — a numbering system that uses only zeros and **ones.**

Bit — an abbreviation for Binary Digit. This is the smallest unit of information a computer circuit can recognise.

Boolean Algebra — the system of algebra developed by mathematician George Boole which uses algebraic notation to express logical relationships (see AND).

Bootstrap — a short program or routine which is read into the computer when it is first turned on. It orients the computer to accept the longer, following program.

Bug — an error in a computer program which stops the program from running properly. Although it is generally used to mean only a fault or an error in a program, the term bug can also be used for a fault in the computer hardware.

Bus — a number of conductors used for transmitting signals such as data instructions, or power in and out of a computer.

Byte — a group of binary digits which make up a computer word. Eight is the most usual number of bits in a byte.

C

CAI — Computer Assisted Instruction.

CAL — Computer Assisted Learning. The term is generally used to describe programs which involve the learner with the learning process.

Chip — the general term for the entire circuit which is etched onto a small piece of silicon. The chip is, of course, at the heart of the microcomputer.

Clock — the timing device within the computer that synchronises its operations.

COBOL — a high level language derived from the words Common Business Orientated Language. COBOL is designed primarily for filing and record-keeping.

Comparator — a device which compares two things and produces a signal related to the difference between the two.

Compiler — a computer program that converts high level programming language into binary machine code so the computer can handle it.

Complement — a number which is derived from another according to specified rules.

Computer — a device with three main abilities or functions:
1) to accept data
2) to solve problems
3) to supply results

CPU — stands for Central Processing Unit. This is the heart of the computer's intelligence, where data is handled and instructions are carried out.

Cursor — a character which appears on the TV screen when the computer is operating. It shows where the next character will be printed. On a computer there are usually 'cursor control keys' to allow the user to move the cursor around the screen.

D

Data — information in a form which the computer can process.

Debug — the general term for going through a program and correcting any errors in it, that is, chasing down and removing bugs (see Bug).

Digital Computer —a computer which operates on information which is in a discrete form.

Disk/Disc — this is a magnetically sensitised plastic disk, a little smaller than a single play record. This is used for storing programs and for obtaining data. Disks are considerably faster to load than a cassette of the same length program. The disk can be searched very quickly while a program is running for additional data.

Display — the visual output of the computer, generally on a TV or monitor screen.

Dot Matrix Printer — a printer which prints either the listing of a program or that which is displayed on the TV screen. Each letter and character is made up of a number of dots. The higher the number of dots per character the finer the resolution of the printer.

Dynamic Memory — a memory unit within the computer which 'forgets' its contents when the power is turned off.

E

Editor — this term is generally used for the routine within the computer which allows you to change lines of a program while you are writing it.

EPROM — stands for Erasable Programmable Read-Only Memory. This is like the ROM in the computer, except that it is fairly easy to load material into an EPROM and it doesn't disappear when you turn the power off. EPROMs must be placed in a strong ultra violet light to erase them.

Error Messages — the information given by a computer where there is a fault in the coding during a part of a program, usually shown by the computer stopping, and printing a word, or a word and numbers, or a combination of numbers only, at the bottom of the screen. This tells you what mistake has been made. Common mistakes include using the letter O instead of zero in a line, or leaving out a pair of brackets, or one of the brackets, in an expression, or failing to define a variable.

F

File — a collection of related items of information organised in a systematic way.

Floppy Disk — a relatively cheap form of magnetic disk used for storing computer information, and so named because it is quite flexible (see Disk/Disc).

Flow Chart — a diagram drawn up before writing a program, in which the main operations are enclosed within rectangles or other shapes and connected by lines, with arrows to represent loops, and decisions written at the branches. It makes writing a program much easier because traps such as infinite loops, or non-defined variables can be caught at an early stage. It may not be worth writing a flow chart for very short programs, but generally a flow chart aids in creating programs.

Firmware — there are three kinds of 'ware' in computers: software 'temporary' programs; hardware like the ROM which contains permanent information; and firmware in which the information is relatively permanent, as in an EPROM (see EPROM).

Flip-Flop — a circuit which maintains one electrical condition until changed to the opposite condition by an input signal.

FORTRAN — an acronym for FORmula TRANslation, this is a high level, problem orientated computer language for scientific and mathematical use.

G

Gate — an electrical circuit which, although it may accept one or more incoming signals, only sends out a single signal.

Graphics — pictorial information as opposed to letters and numbers.

H

Hard Copy — computer output which is in permanent form.

Hardware — the physical parts of the computer (also see software and firmware).

Hexadecimal (Hex) — a numbering system to the base sixteen. The digits zero to nine are used, as well as the letters A, B, C, D, E and F to represent numbers. A equals 10, B equals 11, C equals 12, and so on. Hex is often used by microprocessor users.

Hex Pad — a keyboard designed specifically for entering hexadecimal notation.

High Level Language — a programming language which allows the user to talk to the computer more or less in English. In general, the higher the level of the language (that is, the closer it is to English), the longer it takes for the computer to translate it into a language it can use. Lower level languages are far more difficult for human operators but are generally executed far more quickly.

I

Input — the information fed into the computer via a keyboard, a microphone, a cassette or a disk.

Input/Output (I/O Device) — a device which accepts information or instructions from the outside world, relays it to the computer, and then, after processing, sends the information out in a form suitable for storing, or in a form which could be understood by a human being.

Instruction — data which directs a single step in the processing of information by the computer (also known as a command).

Integrated Circuit — a complete electronic circuit imprinted on a semiconductor surface.

Interface — the boundary between the computer and a peripheral such as a printer.

Interpreter — a program which translates the high level language fed in by the human operator, into a language which the machine can understand.

Inverter — a logic gate that changes the signal being fed in, to the opposite one.

Interactive Routine — part of a program which is repeated over and over again until a specified condition is reached.

J

Jump Instruction — an instruction which tells the computer to go to another part of the program, when the destination of this move depends on the result of a calculation just performed.

K

K — this relates to the size of the memory. Memory is usually measured in 4K blocks. 1K contains 1,024 bytes.

Keyword — the trigger word in a line of programming, usually the first word after the line number. Keywords include STOP, PRINT and GOTO.

L

Language — computer languages are divided into three sections: high level languages, such as BASIC, which are reasonably close to English and fairly easy for humans to use; low level languages, such as Assembler, that use short phrases which have some connection with English (ADD for add and RET for return, for instance); and machine code which communicates more or less directly with the machine.

LCD — this stands for Liquid Crystal Diode. Some computers such as the TRS-80 Pocket Computer use an LCD display.

LED — this stands for Light Emitting Diode. The bright

red numbers which are often used on watch or clock displays are made up of LEDs.

Logic — the mathematical form of a study of relationships between events.

Loop — a sequence of instructions within a program which is performed over and over again until a particular condition is satisfied.

M

Machine Language or Machine Code — an operation code which can be understood and acted upon directly by the computer.

Magnetic Disk — see Disk and Floppy Disk.

Mainframe — computers are generally divided into three groups, and the group a computer falls into depends more or less on its size. The computer you are thinking of buying is a microcomputer; medium sized computers are known as minicomputers; and the giant computers that you sometimes see in science fiction movies are mainframe computers. Until 15 years ago mainframe computers were, in practical terms, the only ones available.

Memory — there are two types of memory within a computer. The first is called ROM (read-only memory); this is the memory that comes already programmed on the computer, which tells the computer how to make decisions and how to carry out arithmetic operations. This memory is unaffected when you turn the computer off. The second type is RAM (random access memory). This memory holds the program you type in at the keyboard or send in via a cassette or disk. In most computers the computer 'forgets' what is in RAM when you turn the power off.

Microprocessor — the heart of any computer. It requires peripheral unit interfaces, such as a power supply and input and output devices, to act as a microcomputer.

MODEM — stands for Modulator Demodulator. This is a device which allows two computers to talk to each other over the telephone. The computers usually use a cradle in which a telephone receiver is placed.

Monitor — this has two meanings in computer terms. One meaning is a television-like display. A monitor has no facility for tuning television programs, and usually the picture produced on a monitor is superior to that produced by an ordinary television. The second meaning of a monitor relates to ROM. The monitor of a computer is described as the information it has built in when you buy it. This information allows it to make decisions and carry out arithmetic computations.

Motherboard — a framework to which extra circuits can be added. These extra circuits often give the computer facilities which are not built-in, such as that of producing sound or of controlling a light pen.

MPU — an abbreviation for Microprocessor Unit.

N

Nano-second — a nano-second is one thousand billionth of a second, the unit of speed in which a computer or a memory chip is often rated.

Non-Volatile Memory — memory which is not lost when the computer is turned off. Some of the smaller computers such as the TRS-80 Pocket Computer have non-volatile memory. The batteries hold the program you enter for several hundred hours.

Not — a Boolean logic operation that changes a binary digit into its opposite.

Null String — a string which contains no characters. It is shown in the program as two double quote marks, without anything between them.

Numeric — pertaining to numbers as opposed to letters (that is, alphabetic). Many keyboards are described as being alphanumeric which means both numbers and letters are provided.

O

Octal — a numbering system which uses eight as the base, and the digits 0, 1, 2, 3, 4, 5, 6 and 7. The Octal system is not used very much nowadays in microcomputer fields. The Hexadecimal system is more common (see Hexadecimal).

Operating System — the software or firmware generally provided with the machine that allows you to run other programs.

OR — an arithmetic operation that returns a 1, if one or more inputs are 1.

Oracle — a method of sending text messages with a broadcast television signal. A teletext set is required to decode the messages. Oracle is run by Independent Television Service in the UK, and a similar service — Ceefax — is provided by the BBC.

Output — information or data fed out by the computer to such devices as a TV-like screen, a printer or a cassette tape. The output usually consists of the information which the computer has produced as a result of running a program.

Overflow — a number too large or too small for the computer to handle.

P

Pad — see Keypad.

Page — often used to refer to the amount of information needed to fill one TV screen, so you can talk about seeing a page of a program, the amount of the listing that will appear on the screen at one time.

PASCAL — a high level language.

Peripheral — anything which is hooked onto a computer, for control by the computer, such as a disk unit, a printer or a voice synthesiser.

Port — a socket through which information can be fed out of or in to a computer.

Prestel — the British telecom name for a system of calling up pages of information from a central computer via the telephone and displaying them on a television screen. A similar commercial version in the United States is known as The Source.

Program — in computer terms program has two meanings. One is the list of instructions that you feed into a computer, and the second is used as a verb, as in 'to program a computer'.

PROM — stands for Programmable Read Only Memory. This is a device which can be programmed, and once it is then the program is permanent (also see EPROM and ROM).

R

Random Access Memory (RAM) — the memory within a computer which can be changed at will by the person using the computer. The contents of RAM are usually lost when a computer is turned off. RAM is the memory device that stores the program that you type in and also stores the results of calculations in progress.

Read-Only Memory (ROM) — in contrast to RAM, information in ROM cannot be changed by the user of the computer, and the information is not lost when the computer is turned off. The data in ROM is put there by the manufacturers and tells the computer how to make decisions and how to carry out arithmetic computations. The size of ROM and RAM is given in the unit K (see K).

Recursion — the continuous repetition of a part of the program.

Register — a specific place in the memory where one or more computer words are stored during operations.

Reserved Word — a word that you cannot use for a variable in a program because the computer will read it as something else. An example is the word TO. Because TO has a specific computer meaning, most computers will reject it as a name for a variable. The same goes for words like FOR, GOTO and STOP.

Routine — this word can be used as a synonym for program, or can refer to a specific section within a program (also see Subroutine).

S

Second Generation — this has two meanings. The first applies to computers using transistors, as opposed to first generation computers which used valves. Second generation can also mean the second copy of a particular program; subsequent generations are degraded by more and more noise.

Semiconductor — a material that is usually an electrical insulator but under specific conditions can become a conductor.

Serial — information which is stored or sent in a sequence, one bit at a time.

Signal — an electrical pulse which is a conveyor of data.

Silicon Valley — the popular name given to an area in California where many semiconductor manufacturers are located.

SNOBOL — a high level language.

Software — the program which is entered into the computer by a user which tells the computer what to do.

Software Compatible — this refers to two different computers which can accept programs written for the other.

Static Memory — a non-volatile memory device which retains information so long as the power is turned on, but does not require additional boosts of power to keep the memory in place.

Subroutine — part of a program which is often accessed many times during the execution of the main program. A subroutine ends with an instruction to go back to the line after the one which sent it to the subroutine.

T

Teletext — information transmitted in the top section of a broadcast television picture. It requires a special set to decode it to fill the screen with text information. The BBC service is known as Ceefax, the ITV service as Oracle. Teletext messages can also be transmitted by cable, for example the Prestel service in Britain or The Source in the United States.

Teletype — a device like a typewriter which can send information and also receive and print it.

Terminal — a unit independent of the central processing unit. It generally consists of a keyboard and a cathode ray display.

Time Sharing — a process by which a number of users may have access to a large computer which switches rapidly from one user to another in sequence, so each user is under the impression that he or she is the sole user of the computer at that time.

Truth Table — a mathematical table which lists all the possible results of a Boolean logic operation, showing the results you get from various combinations of inputs.

U

UHF — Ultra High Frequency (300-3000 megaHertz).

Ultra Violet Erasing — Ultra violet light must be used to erase EPROMs (see EPROM).

V

Variable — a letter or combination of letters and symbols which the computer can assign to a value or a word during the run of a program.

VDU — an abbreviation for Visual Display Unit.

Volatile — refers to memory which 'forgets' its contents when the power is turned off.

W

Word — a group of characters, or a series of binary digits, which represent a unit of information and occupy a single storage location. The computer processes a word as a single instruction.

Word-Processor — a highly intelligent typewriter which allows the typist to manipulate text, to move it around, to justify margins and to shift whole paragraphs if necessary on a screen before outputting the information onto a printer. Word-processors usually have memories, so that standard letters and the text of letters, written earlier, can be stored.

BIBLIOGRAPHY

Compiled by Tim Hartnell

The A to Z Book of Computer Games (McIntire, Thomas C, Tab Books, Blue Ridge Summit, Pa.).

This is a fine Tab book to give you program ideas and ready-to-run programs, although some of the games are a disappointment, such as the overly long Othello program which does not even play, but simply records the moves made by two human players. Others, however, such as Fivecard and Hotshot, are well written, and well worth entering into your microcomputer.

BASIC Computer Games (ed. Ahl, David, Creative Computing Press, Morristown, New Jersey).

This is a classic work, the source of more programming ideas than any other computer games book ever published. I had a meal with David Ahl one night in London after a PCW show and discussed the book. He said that he'd been in the personal computer field almost before there were personal computers, and while many of the games in this book do not seem startling now, the fact that people could write and play games for computer interaction at all seemed quite incredible in the late seventies. The Checkers program, and Life for Two are just a couple of the treasures you will find in this splendid program and idea source book.

BASIC Computer Programs for the Home (Sternberg, Charles D, Hayden Book Company, Inc., Rochelle Park, New Jersey).

Traditionally, home computers (when first purchased) have been used for playing games. One reason why they have not been used for more serious applications stems from the lack of a readily available, comprehensive set of home applications programs that were easy to use and understand and that satisfied the practical requirements of the home. This book provides a set of programs to make your computer start earning its keep. The programs provide a good cross-section of practical applications; these have been designed so as not to rely upon the availability of tape or disk-storage devices. The programs cover a wide field, and are divided into a number of sections: home financial programs (including household expenses and income tax recording); car related programs (including fuel use and trip planning); 'Kitchen Helpmates' (including diet and meal planning programs); scheduling programs for home use (including a reminder calendar and a couple of programs which I imagine are designed to short circuit arguments about which television programs will be watched); and 'List programs for every purpose' (including Christmas cards, music collections and three versions of an addresses program).

The BASIC Handbook (Lien, David A, Compusoft Publishing, San Diego, California).

This is an encyclopedia of the BASIC language. Now that BASIC is so firmly established throughout the microcomputer world, it is necessary to make its many dialects understandable so that programs can be transported between different computers. When you have found exactly the program you've been looking for, it is very frustrating to be unable to run it on your computer. This book addresses that problem by discussing in detail just about every commonly used BASIC statement, function, operator and command. For the most part, BASIC words mean the same thing to every computer which recognises them. If a computer does not possess the capabilities of a needed or specified word, there are often ways to accomplish the same function by using another word, or combination of words. Although the handbook requires some

117

application to transform the information into usable form, it is a very valuable reference work indeed. Every BASIC word you have ever heard of (and many you may not have heard of, such as LE, NE, GOTO-OF, RES and TIME) is probably in the book. It may be of limited use to you in your early days of computing, but it should become an indispensable handbook once you get more involved in the subject.

Beat the Odds, Microcomputer Simulations of Casino Games (Sagan, Hans, Hayden Book Company, Inc., Rochelle Park, New Jersey).

The book explains how to play certain casino games (trente-et-quarante, roulette, chemin-de-fer, craps and blackjack) and gives complete program listings in BASIC with commentaries on systems and optimal strategies. Professor Sagan (Professor of Mathematics at North Carolina State University) says he wrote the book in an attempt to convince people that, in the long run, they could not win — except possibly at blackjack — and to explain some popular systems and their pitfalls, and above all to provide very realistic computer simulations of the games themselves. He has succeeded in his attempt. The listings are possibly longer than other computer versions of the same games, but this is because the Sagan versions strictly duplicate the odds involved in playing the game 'in real life', and cover all the eventualities that a real game can produce. The programs are well-structured, and an examination of the listings should give you ideas for improving your own programming.

Beginner's Guide to Chess (Keene, Raymond, Pelham Books Ltd, London).

An ideal guide to simple chess-playing techniques which you can turn into algorithms if you intend to write a chess program of your own.

The Calculator Game Book for Kids of All Ages (Hartman, Arlene, Signet Books, New York).

The book's title says it all, and the names of the games

(which include Fibonacci Follies, Stretch to Sixty and Casting Out 9s) suggest the book's contents. There are some worthwhile brain-stretching puzzles, and 15 or so ideas definitely calling for conversion to computer games.

33 Challenging Computer Games for TRS-80/Apple/PET (Chance, David, Tab Books, Blue Ridge Summit, Pa.).

Even if you don't have any of the three computers named in the title, you will still find the book a goldmine of ideas for your own development, and many of them will run, with minimal alteration, on any BASIC-using computer. Particularly commendable programs are Life Support, Scrambled Eggs and Tank Assault.

Communicating with Microcomputers (Witten, Ian H., Academic Press, London).

This is an introduction to the technology of man/computer communications for the non-specialist. By placing particular emphasis on low-cost techniques associated with small systems and personal computers, the reader's attention is focused on the positive nature of the 'microprocessor revolution' — how machines can help people — rather than the negative aspects which are often highlighted in the non-technical press. The level of the book is suitable for the layman with some acquaintance with electronics. The final section, on speech communication, provides the most fascinating reading.

Computer Appreciation (Fry, T.F., Newnes, Butterworths, 1975).

A fairly 'straight' but useful overview of computer operation, and business applications. Designed to be used as a text for a course of business studies, the book covers a wide range of topics from a short account of the historical development of calculating devices, through computer hardware and programming, to the organisation of a modern data-processing department. It concludes with a brief consideration of the applications of computers and a discussion on the effects of computers upon management matters. It is surprisingly undated, despite the extraordinary increase in hardware availability and capability since the book was written.

The Computer Book: An Introduction to Computers and Computing (Bradbeer, Robin; De Bono, Peter; Laurie, Peter; BBC Publications).

This book was published in conjunction with the BBC television series 'The Computer Programme', first transmitted on BBC2 from January 1982, and produced by Paul Kriwaczek. I discussed this book with Robin Bradbeer while it was being written, and he told me that the BBC editors were ruthless in pointing out any use of jargon. They insisted, said Robin, that nothing could be taken for granted. This insistence has resulted in a book which anyone can understand. It assumes nothing, not even the knowledge of how to use a shift key — or the effect of using it — on a typewriter. The many illustrations and photographs break up the text, which gives a detailed introduction to computers, especially micros, and their possible applications.

Computer Games for Businesses, Schools and Homes (Nahigian, J Victor and Hodges, William S. Winthrop Publishers Inc., Cambridge, Mass.).

Some of the programs are a little thin for the size and price of the book, but the best ones are well worth adapting to run on your computer. The inclusion of long, clear sample run printouts ensures that you know exactly what the programs will do before you run them. The Tennis and Star Trek programs are especially good.

Dice Games Old and New (Tredd, William E., Oleander Press, Cambridge).

This will give you enough clearly written games

explanations to keep you creating games programs on your microcomputer for a long time to come.

The Electronic Calculator in Business, Home and School (Birtwistle, Claude, Elliot Right Way Books, Kingswood, Surrey).

To get the best out of a calculator, you need to understand the mathematics which lies behind the operations. That is the purpose of the book, and in general it succeeds in this aim. The maths involved is, however, fairly simple and basic, since the book was written with a wide range of people in mind — the pupil at school, the student at college, the business person and the householder. It is a practical book which should be read and worked through with a calculator to hand.

Everyman's Indoor Games (Brandreth, Gyles, J M Dent and Sons Ltd, London).

If you're looking for games to convert into computer programs, ignore the chapters entitled Parlour Games and Children's Party Games and stick to the rest of the book, a treasure trove of games concepts which are certainly worth using as a starting point. Fox and Geese, Poker Dice and Billiards, as described in the book, are only a few of the programs you might write after reading it.

Games and Puzzles for Addicts (Millington, Roger, M and J Hobbs, Walton-on-Thames).

These games and puzzles first appeared in the weekly computer news-magazine 'Datalink', so they are especially likely to appeal to computer buffs. There are many ideas here that can be converted into games to be played with the computer.

Games for Home, Travel and Parties (Jensen, Helen, Western Publishing Company Inc., Racine, Wisconsin).

Aimed squarely at children, this book gives some games which are simple to program (these include Snakes, Lift-Off and Fish), and contains a complete chapter on how to play chess.

Home Computers, Questions and Answers, Hardware (Didday, Rich, dilithium Press).

The book has two main purposes. Firstly, it is intended to give readers a real feeling for what is involved in home computing, so that they can make rational decisions before buying equipment. Secondly, it is intended to give people who have no specialised knowledge of computing a general background to the subject, and specifically to microcomputers. The book succeeds in imparting enough information to ensure you will have little trouble understanding articles about advanced projects in computer hobbyist magazines, advertisements for home computing equipment, or other people who do have advanced computer knowledge.

Inside BASIC Games (Mateosian, Richard, Sybex).

This book is a guide, albeit a slightly overwritten one, for anyone who wishes to understand computer games. You will learn how to write interactive programs in BASIC and how the principles of systems development are applied to small computers. The book also looks at how the features of specific small computer systems have been supported in BASIC. The sections of the book include: Arithmetic Games, Guessing Games, Time Games, Date Games, Taxman, and programming in 'Free BASIC', a structured BASIC that is translated manually into the actual BASIC instructions to be entered into the computer. Free BASIC is not a language; it is a program description medium (like flowcharts) that has no line numbers, and uses symbolic names for subroutines. Additional chapters look at The Match-Up Game, Craps and Alien Life. If you can contend with the verbiage, you will find this book well worthwhile.

An Introduction to Personal and Business Computing (Zaks, Rodnay, Sybex).

I had lunch with Rodnay in London during a PCW show and he told me that he thought current American predictions on the growth of the personal computer field were grossly pessimistic. He pointed out that the predictions current in 1978, when he wrote this book, have been proved so inaccurate that would-be prophets should take warning and assume that whatever they say will be wrong by a factor of 10 or 100. Despite its age — and computer books do age uncommonly quickly — this book is a good introduction to the field, explaining in clear, snappy English the fundamentals of computer operation. Dr Zaks also gives suggestions on what to look for when buying a computer.

Microsoft BASIC (Knecht, Ken, dilithium Press, Forest Grove, Oregon).

This book presents a complete introduction to programming in Microsoft BASIC. The concepts presented are illustrated with short, working programs. By starting with the simplest and most commonly used commands, and then progressing on to the more complex BASIC commands, Mr Knecht shows how the more powerful versions of the language can save valuable programming time and effort.

The Personal Computer Book (Bradbeer, Robin, Input Two-Nine).

The title says it all. Robin is deeply involved in the microfield in Great Britain. He started the North London Polytechnic Computer Fairs, assisted the BBC with their microcomputer television show (and co-authored *The Computer Book*, published by the BBC), and edited the monthly publication *Educational Computing*. This gave him a strong background from which to write the book. It explains what a computer is and how it works; it elucidates the mysteries inside the 'black boxes' which make up a computer; and it gives a number of very useful appendices, including bus standards, manufacturers and distributors, magazines, a selected bibliography (compiled by Richard Ross-Langley, of *Mine of Information*) and a glossary. But perhaps the most interesting and useful section of the book is the part which describes, in some detail, the majority of computer systems available on the British market, their price and their capabilities. Overall, this is a very impressive source book.

Personal Computers: What They Are and How to Use Them (Wels, Byron G., Trafalgar House Publishing).

A great deal has happened in the computer world since this book was written in 1978, but there is still a great deal of value and interest in it. The book details some of the personal computers available, and the improvements that are likely to be made in the future. It explains, in layman terms, how a computer works, and how to make it work for you. There is also material on the construction and maintenance of small computer systems.

Play the Game (Love, Brian, Michael Joseph and Ebury Press, London).

This is a splendid book, containing 40 or so full-size reproductions of Victorian (and pre-Victorian) board games, many suitable for playing against a computer. It is even possible to use the boards in the book (the computer then tells you where it is moving on this external board) rather than write a routine within the program to display a board.

The Pocket Calculator Games Book (Schlossberg, Edwin and Brockman, John, Wilton House Publications Ltd., London).

There are many ideas here suitable for conversion into computer games.

57 Practical Programs and Games in BASIC (Tracton, Ken, Tab Books, Blue Ridge Summit, Pa.).

There are more serious programs than games (of the Chi-Square Evaluation and Fibonacci Numbers variety) in this book. They are well-programmed, and supported by adequate (if brief) documentation, and by flow-charts. The Space Wars programs (versions one and two) at the end of the book are particularly good.

Problems for Computer Solution (Rogowski, Stephen J, Creative Computing Press, Morristown, New Jersey).

This outlines over 50 simple (and a few not-so-simple) problems which can be solved by writing a program. There are both teacher and student editions of this book; the teacher edition has a suggested program and sample run printout to solve the difficulty. It is an excellent source for educational ideas.

Stimulating Simulations (Engel, C.W., Hayden Book Company, Inc., New Jersey).

Here, according to the cover, are '12 unique programs in BASIC for the computer hobbyist'. Inside you will find some fascinating programs: Forest Fire, Rare Birds and The Devil's Dungeon are three you are sure to enjoy playing, while Diamond Thief (the computer decides who has committed the crime, then challenges you to discover which of the suspects is guilty) is both well written and tightly programmed.

TAKE TWO! 32 Board Games for 2 Players (Tapson, Frank, A & C Black, London).

This book is aimed at children, but it does give many fascinating ideas that could be transformed into computer games (even if some of them are duplicated elsewhere in the book).

24 Tested, Ready-to-Run Game Programs in BASIC (Tracton, Ken, Tab Books, Blue Ridge Summit, Pa.).

Tab Books are prolific publishers in the microcomputer program field, and their books are deservedly successful. If nothing else, reading a book such as this one will give you ideas for structuring programs neatly, and for writing them to ensure the maximum compatibility between different versions of BASIC. Many of the games, such as Auto Rally and Capture the Alien, are (despite their weak titles) well thought out, carefully constructed programs.

1001 Things to Do with Your Personal Computer (Sawush, Mark, Tab Books, Blue Ridge Summit, Pa.).

I bought this book at a computer fair in Atlanta, and

read it (making notes, and turning down page corners) on the flight to London. And I still hadn't finished it on arrival. If you feel you have come to the end of possible applications for your computer, buy this book and discover that you have barely scratched the surface. It tells you about writing music and stories, aiding a mechanic or a carpenter, solving simultaneous equations, astrology, and much, much more.

The World Computer Chess Championship (Hayes, Jean E., and Levy, David N.L., Edinburgh University Press, Edinburgh).

This is a fascinating account of the world's first machine versus machine chess championship, held in 1974, when the dozen or so computer programs taking part were the only chess programs in existence. The games are analysed in detail, and the final section of the book outlines a board-numbering system which you could use if you're considering writing your own chess program. The book makes you realise how far the computer world has come in only a few years.